Become a Li...
the Divine Light

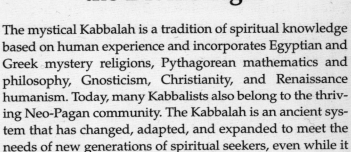

The mystical Kabbalah is a tradition of spiritual knowledge based on human experience and incorporates Egyptian and Greek mystery religions, Pythagorean mathematics and philosophy, Gnosticism, Christianity, and Renaissance humanism. Today, many Kabbalists also belong to the thriving Neo-Pagan community. The Kabbalah is an ancient system that has changed, adapted, and expanded to meet the needs of new generations of spiritual seekers, even while it retains the basic divine truths at its core.

If you feel a growing desire for a type of spirituality that is more personal, accessible, and tangible, then the mystical Kabbalah could be for you. One of the oldest and finest systems for bringing out the latent psychic gifts that reside within us all, the Kabbalah is a practical system of spiritual development, self-empowerment, and personal growth.

The power of the Kabbalah can be experienced in ways that will help facilitate spiritual growth and awareness. One way is to visualize the spheres of the Tree of Life as they exist within the human body using what is called the Middle Pillar exercise. Perhaps the most effective tool for swift comprehension of the Kabbalah is through the innovative ritual drama called Tree Walking—revealed here for the first time!

The Kabbalah of today is a dynamic philosophy that includes theories on the birth of the universe, the Eternal Mind of God, and the spiritual development of humanity. It is a precise mystical system that outlines Universal Laws and shows us how to make use of spiritual principles in everyday life. There is simply no better system for attaining peace, balance, and wisdom in the Western tradition.

About the Authors

Chic and Tabatha Cicero are Senior Adepts of the Hermetic Order of the Golden Dawn. They share an enthusiasm for the esoteric arts. They live in Florida with their cat, Lealah, where they work and practice magic.

To Write to the Authors

If you wish to contact the authors or would like more information about this book, please write to the authors in care of Llewellyn Worldwide and we will forward your request. Both the authors and publisher appreciate hearing from you and learning of your enjoyment of this book and how it has helped you. Llewellyn Worldwide cannot guarantee that every letter written to the authors can be answered, but all will be forwarded. Please write to:

Chic Cicero and Sandra Tabatha Cicero
c/o Llewellyn Worldwide
P.O. Box 64383, Dept. K138–4
St. Paul, MN 55164-0383, U.S.A.

Please enclose a self-addressed, stamped envelope for reply, or $1.00 to cover costs.
If outside the U.S.A., enclose international postal reply coupon.

A SIMPLE GUIDE TO SPIRITUAL WHOLENESS

EXPERIENCING
THE
KABBALAH

CHIC CICERO
SANDRA TABATHA CICERO

1997
Llewellyn Publications
St. Paul, Minnesota 55164-0383, U.S.A.

Experiencing the Kabbalah © 1997 by Chic Cicero and Sandra Tabatha Cicero. All rights reserved. No part of this book may be reproduced in any manner whatsoever without the written permission from Llewellyn Publications, except in the case of brief quotations embodied in critical articles and reviews.

FIRST EDITION
First Printing

Cover art and design by Tom Grewe
Illustrations on pages 15, 19, 21, 23, 25, 27, 211, and 213
     by Sandra Tabatha Cicero
Illustrations on pages 57, 61, 69, 75, 83, 89, 97, 103, 109, 117,
     and 123 by Nyease Somersett
Editing and layout by Sandra Tabatha Cicero
Project management by Jan Feeney

Library of Congress Cataloging-in-Publication Data
Cicero, Chic, 1936–
     Experiencing the Kabbalah: a simple guide to spiritual
wholeness/Chic Cicero, Sandra Tabatha Cicero.
          p. cm.
     Includes bibliographical references and index.
     ISBN 1–56718–138–4 (trade paper)
     1. Spiritual life. 2. Cabala. I. Cicero, Sandra Tabatha, 1959–
. II. Title.
BL624.C497 1997
296.7' 12--dc21   97-24732
                                                                        CIP
Llewellyn Worldwide does not participate in, endorse, or have any authority or responsibility concerning private business transactions between our authors and the public. All mail addressed to the author is forwarded but the publisher cannot, unless specifically instructed by the author, give out an address or phone number.

Llewellyn Publications
A Division of Llewellyn Worldwide, Ltd.
P.O. Box 64383, Dept. K138-4
St. Paul, Minnesota 55164-0383, U.S.A.

For Adam and Isidora Forrest
and fellow Tree Walkers everywhere,
and in memory of
The Grinch

Also by the Authors

The Golden Dawn Magical System Kit
  including:
  The New Golden Dawn Ritual Tarot (deck)
  The New Golden Dawn Ritual Tarot (book)
  Layout Sheet
Secrets of a Golden Dawn Temple
Self-Initiation into the Golden Dawn Tradition
The Golden Dawn Journal Series
  including:
  Book I: Divination
  Book II: Qabalah: Theory and Magic
  Book III: The Art of Hermes

Forthcoming

The Magical Pantheons
  (The Golden Dawn Journal: Book IV)
The Middle Pillar (Third Edition)

Table of Contents

27th, Peh; The 26th Path, Ayin; The 25th Path, Semekh; The 24th Path, Nun; The 23rd Path, Mem; The 22nd Path, Lamed; The 21st Path, Kaph; The 20th Path, Yod; The 19th Path, Teth; The 18th Path, Cheth; The 17th Path, Zayin; The 16th Path, Vav; The 15th Path, Heh; The 14th Path, Daleth; The 13th Path, Gimel; The 12th Path, Beth; The 11th Path, Aleph

Chapter Five: A Tree Walk with the Paths 183

The Path Stations; After Malkuth; The Address of the 32nd Path; After Yesod; The Address of the 31st Path; The Address of the 30th Path; After Hod; The Address of the 29th Path; The Address of the 28th Path; The Address of the 27th Path; After Hod; The Address of the 26th Path; The Address of the 25th Path; The Address of the 24th Path; After Tiphareth; The Address of the 23rd Path; The Address of the 22nd Path; After Geburah; The Address of the 21st Path; The Address of the 20th Path; The Address of the 19th Path; After Chesed; The Address of the 18th Path; The Address of the 17th Path; After the 17th Path; The Address of Daath; After Binah; The Address of the 16th Path; The Address of the 15th Path; The Address of the 14th Path; After Chokmah; The Address of the 13th Path; The Address of the 12th Path; The Address of the 11th Path

Chapter Six: The Tree Within Us 209

Vibration; The Middle Pillar; The Middle Pillar Exercise; Appendix to the Middle Pillar; Uses of the Middle Pillar; A Simplified Middle Pillar; Working with Archangels; The Archangelic Middle Pillar; Color Visualization Techniques; The Exercise of the Three Pillars; Advanced Color Workings; Archangels and Their Colors; The Tree Walk; A Guided Visualization; Affirmations

List of Figures and Illustrations

INTRODUCTION

The idea for writing this book came about one day as we finished giving a lecture on the Kabbalah, followed by a ritual drama called "The Tree Walk" which was designed as an informative and entertaining way to teach students how to understand basic Kabbalistic concepts—not in the usual abstruse language that many books on the subject are written in, but rather in a theatrical performance wherein the audience interacts with actors or ritualists who represent Kabbalistic ideas. A friend of ours, who had been giving classes on the Kabbalah, suggested that our scripted version of "The Tree Walk," which we had been performing for a number of years, would be an excellent teaching tool for showing beginning students how to relate to the Kabbalah in human terms and apply its ancient wisdom to everyday life in the modern

world. Many books on the subject are either too simplified or too advanced, and in both cases the beginner is still left with a system that is very abstract and
hard to grasp on an experiential level. It would be a
shame if students who truly wished to understand
the Kabbalah were unable to do so simply because
they could not personally relate to its ideas as delin-
eated in the usual texts. This does not have to be,
and should not be, the case.

In the minds of many individuals who study the
magic and mysticism of the western world, there is
simply no better system for spiritual growth and personal evolution than that of the Kabbalah. No other
system that we are aware of is as symmetrical, beautiful, harmonious, all-encompassing, or better suited to
the psychology of the Western mind. Yet this elegant
system of mystical knowledge, which was in past
ages reserved only for a select few among the ancient
Hebrews, is now being discovered by spiritual seekers from all walks of life and from every conceivable
religious faith and ethnic background—Eastern as
well as Western. Kabbalistic knowledge has never
been a static, rigid body of teachings; it has always
been an ancient river of collective wisdom, fed by several smaller tributaries and streams of personal
insight, creativity, and experience. The Kabbalah of
today has become far less sectarian and much more
universal in scope.

It is our hope that this book can provide the
reader who is new to the subject with exactly this type

of personal, hands-on experience with the Kabbalah. It doesn't matter whether the reader intends to make the Kabbalah his or her primary spiritual focus, or merely has a passing curiosity about it. Students from all spiritual paths should be able to benefit in some way from the vast amount of wisdom represented by the Kabbalah.

As a final note, readers should be aware that the English transliteration of the Hebrew word Kabbalah is often spelled differently. Variations in spelling include Qabalah, Qabala, Cabala, and even Quabbalah. Some authors use the different spellings of the word to denote different Kabbalistic traditions. For example, the spelling of Kabbalah is often used by orthodox Jews to represent a more orthodox form of these ancient teachings. Western ceremonial magicians often prefer the spelling of Qabalah to indicate a more Hermetic or magical form of the system. Although we, too, favor the spelling of Qabalah, here we have opted for the more traditional spelling of Kabbalah to indicate an extensive system that encompasses all forms and branches of this mystical tradition—from ancient times to the modern era.

The Kabbalah of today is accessible to anyone who wishes to study it. But studying books is not enough. Ritual exercises, meditations, visualizations, and daily affirmations are among the tools that will help readers internalize Kabbalistic knowledge. Students who use these tools will soon discover the

Kabbalah to be a deep and unending well of divine wisdom, creativity, peace, and inspiration—the full potential of which has yet to be reached.

— Chic Cicero
Sandra Tabatha Cicero
Metatron House
Summer Solstice 1997

CHAPTER ONE

THE KABBALAH

The Tree is a symbol for spiritual growth that has existed in one form or another in virtually all mystical traditions and cultures. In ancient Mesopotamia, the *hom* or central Tree of Life was said to stand in the middle of the Sacred Grove of the Gods. In Teutonic mythology, the cosmic tree known as *Yggdrasil* extended from the heavens to the very core of the earth. The *Arbor Vitae* can often be found in the art of the Orient. But the most sublime use of the Tree as an image for spiritual evolution is undoubtedly that of the *Tree of Life* from the Kabbalah. It is from the ancient and fertile soil of the Hebrew tradition that the Kabbalistic Tree of Life takes root.

Most of the world's major religions teach that all humans will return to the primal source from whence we came. But these same religions often do not provide instruction (other than moral admonishments and

1

dogma) on how humans can actively aid their own spiritual progress. They do not provide the exercises, knowledge, training, or any of the practical methods needed for the average human being to facilitate his or her own latent psychic gifts and to accelerate natural spiritual evolution—all the things that are needed to bring these numinous divine gifts into every aspect of daily existence. In modern times there is a growing desire for something more satisfying than the parental advice of "do this and don't do that" —a phrase that used to be effective for the major religions in ages past when people were less educated. The time for blind acceptance of everything that the orthodox institutions say and do is long past. Nowadays, many people are experiencing a growing desire for a type of spirituality that is more personal, accessible, and tangible—a spirituality that is more whole. That is why so many people are turning to the mystical traditions of the East (Buddhism and Hinduism) as well as to those of the West—namely the Kabbalah, along with its main symbol, the Tree of Life.

The mystical Kabbalah is one of the best esoteric systems ever devised for providing this kind of interactive spirituality. It is one of the oldest and finest systems available for bringing out the latent psychic gifts that reside within us all. It is a very practical system that contains several different layers of working. In other words, students of Kabbalah can delve into its mysteries and its knowledge as deeply as they want to—beginners can stay at introductory levels of working, while advanced practitioners can move on to ever-increasing degrees of knowledge and discipline. As one writer stated:

> *The Qabalah, or traditional science of the Hebrews, might be called the mathematics of human thought. It is the algebra of faith. It solves all problems of the soul as equations, by isolating the unknowns. It gives to ideas the clarity and rigorous exactitude of numbers; its results, for the mind, are infallibility (always relative, however, to the sphere of human knowledge) and for the heart, profound peace.*[1]

The Kabbalah

Kabbalah is a Hebrew word that means "tradition." It is derived from the root word *qibel*, meaning "to receive." This refers to the ancient custom of handing down esoteric knowledge by oral transmission. What the word *Kabbalah* encompasses is an entire body of ancient Hebrew mystical principles that are the cornerstone and focus of the Western Esoteric Tradition. This system is ideally suited to the logical, rational mind of Western-thinking people, because it permits us a view of the organization and construction of the universal energies that influence all areas of our lives. We Westerners are raised in an environment that is conducive to rational thought-processes and left-brain activity. The mystical Kabbalah engages this natural predisposition while at the same time activating those intuitive, right-brain faculties within us.

Virtually all Western spiritual systems can trace their roots back to the Kabbalistic Tree of Life. The exact origins of the Kabbalah are unclear, but it certainly contains some vestiges of Egyptian, Greek, and Chaldean influence. According to Hebrew legend, the Kabbalah was first communicated to humanity by the Archangel Metatron, who gave knowledge of it to Adam. This knowledge, so it goes, was then passed on to Noah, Abraham, and Moses. And in the New Testament, Jesus makes several references to Kabbalistic teachings.

The modern Kabbalah is sometimes called the *Hermetic* Kabbalah (after Hermes, the Greek god of wisdom). This Kabbalah is not just for those of Jewish heritage. It is for students of *all* backgrounds and beliefs. The Hermetic Kabbalah is an amalgam of the Hebrew Kabbalah, the Egyptian mystery religion, the mathematical and mystical teachings of Pythagoras, and the beliefs of the Renaissance humanists—many of whom were Christians. Today, many Kabbalists also belong to the thriving Neopagan community. Thus, even though the roots of the Kabbalah are indeed ancient, down through the ages the system has changed, adapted, and expanded to meet the needs of new generations of spiritual seekers, even while it retains its basic divine truths. It has never remained stagnant. This is the hallmark of a *living system* that truly encompasses all areas of human life.

Kabbalah is *not* a philosophy or a religion, although it includes certain attributes of both. Kabbalah is a blueprint that can be used for building a solid foundation of mystical experience. It can provide the student with the means to obtain the stimulus, energy, and validation needed for personal evolution. Through its use, our own natural gifts are enhanced.

By its nature, mysticism is knowledge that cannot be communicated directly, but may be expressed only through symbolism and metaphor. Like other esoteric systems, Kabbalah also draws upon the mystic's awareness of the transcendence of the eternal deity. Another element of Kabbalah is that of *theosophy*, which seeks to reveal the hidden mysteries of the Divine as well as the relationships between the divine life on one hand, and the life of humans on the other. The goal of the Qabalist is to discover and invent keys to the understanding of arcane symbols that reflect the eternal mysteries.

Israel Regardie stated, *"Kabbalah is a trustworthy guide, leading to a comprehension of the Universe and one's own self."* It is all this and more. This "Tradition" was never restricted to instruction in the mystical path; it also includes ideas on the origins of the universe, of angelic hierarchies and the practice of magic. Kabbalah lays the foundation on which the art of magic rests. Magic has been defined by Aleister Crowley as "the science and art of causing change to occur in conformity with Will." To this Dion Fortune added "changes in consciousness."

The Kabbalah, which Dion Fortune called "the Yoga of the West," reveals the nature of certain physical and psychological phenomena. Once these are rightly understood, the student can use the principles of magic to exercise control over the conditions and circumstances of his/her life. Magic provides the practical application of the theories supplied by the Kabbalah.

The Kabbalah is a *twofold* blueprint of the universe. In one aspect it shows us how the manifest universe was created. But in another aspect, it shows how the universal energies manifest within each individual human soul. This is what is known as the *Macrocosm* (the Greater Universe) and the *Microcosm* (the Lesser Universe, which is humanity). One of the most extraordinary things about the Kabbalah is that it provides us with information for interaction between these two universes. This is often expressed by the Hermetic axiom of "As above, so Below." What these two universes represent is successive, interconnected levels of consciousness—the greater divine consciousness of deity, and the lesser consciousness of humankind. With the Kabbalah we can explore cosmic principles and trace their influences within our lives and within our psychic make-up. And by being able to organize and sort out these energies, we can examine them and expand our comprehension of how they function in the world of humanity. We can then focus these forces and use them more constructively to our advantage in all areas of life.

The Kabbalah as it exists today is a vibrant, living, growing, and dynamic system that includes the origin of the entire cosmos, the eternal mind of God, and the spiritual development of humankind. It is a precise mystical system that describes universal laws and shows us how to utilize spiritual principles in everyday life. The mystical Kabbalah is flexible enough to be adapted to each individual's specific needs and stage of development, while retaining its fundamental structure and composition.[2] By firmly fixing the Kabbalistic symbols such as the Tree of Life in one's mind, the student has access to a balanced group of archetypes that the Inner Self can more easily relate to, thus making true spiritual growth more readily attainable. As the student begins to contemplate and experience the energies of the *Sephiroth* (the ten emanations of the Kabbalistic Tree of Life) he or she will find that they develop into genuine forces that become animated within the psyche. These newly awakened forces will initiate a process of reorganization in the mind of the student, gathering up disjointed elements of the divine powers that lay dormant in the average person. They begin to structure themselves in accordance with the Sephiroth, permitting the student to tap into a previously unknown source of divine inspiration which is kept alive and prolific through meditation and active ritual work. The Kabbalah has often been called the "Ladder of Lights" because it not only depicts cosmic generation, which is the descent of the Divine into the physical, but also defines how the individual may employ it for spiritual ascent by purifying both body and mind through ceremony, contemplation, and prayer, until at length one achieves that pristine state of consciousness that is necessary to attain union with the Higher Self—the emissary to the Divine Self represented by the first Sephirah of Kether.

Sometimes beginners are put off by the Kabbalah because they are under the impression that it is too complex. They do not understand why it is necessary to know and understand a few Hebrew words or memorize Kabbalistic correspondences. Yet most people are perfectly willing to learn complex terminology for a variety of different careers, such as engineering, medicine, or law. If our secular jobs are important enough to warrant training on our part, our spiritual evolution deserves the same consideration.

Some people who have a brief encounter with the Kabbalah come away with the idea that it is a purely patriarchal or male-oriented philosophy simply because of its Hebrew origins. Nothing could be further from the truth. Take for example a word that is common throughout Kabbalistic teachings, *Elohim*. This is a word formed from a feminine noun, *Eloah,* and a masculine plural, *im*. You are left with a word that has both male and female characteristics, which literally means "gods"—the creative principle formed from the perfect and equal union of the divine male and the divine female principles. Read in this context, the Kabbalistic origins of the first five books of the Old Testament (*the Pentateuch*) give an entirely new meaning. The first sentence of Genesis, which in Hebrew begins as *"Berashith bara Elohim Ath-ha-Shamaim w'Ath ha-Aretz,"* can be interpreted as "In the beginning, the gods (the united male and female aspects of the Divine) created the Heavens and the Earth." This idea of the equality of the divine male and divine female principles, although suppressed for centuries by male-dominated societies, is carefully hidden in Kabbalistic doctrine, although at times it has slipped out unforeseen in most all translations of the Pentateuch, such as in Genesis 1:26 and 1:27: "And God went on to say let us make man in *our* image, according to our likeness," "And God proceeded to create the man in his image, in God's image he created him; *male and female* he created them."

Another example is the word *Sephiroth*, which is used to describe the ten emanations of the Divine. Here we have a feminine noun *Sephirah* being joined to a feminine plural *oth*. This again points to the importance of the feminine in Kabbalah. The Sephiroth themselves are generally considered feminine because they give form to the emanations of deity. Thus anyone who seriously studies the Kabbalah for any length of time will see that it is a very balanced system for spiritual growth.

The Kabbalah is usually classified under four heads that overlap each other in some instances. They are:

1. *The Dogmatic Kabbalah*—the study of ancient Kabbalistic books.

2. *The Practical Kabbalah*—deals with the construction of talismans in ceremonial magic.

3. *The Literal Kabbalah*—deals with Gematria—the relationships between numbers and the letters of the Hebrew alphabet, which yield many hidden meanings of Hebrew words and names.

4. *The Unwritten Kabbalah*—refers to the correct knowledge of the sacred symbol known as the *Tree of Life* (Etz ha-Chayim).

We will not at this time describe the long history and evolution of the Kabbalah as elucidated by various teachers and sources down through the ages. To do so would be to place an undue burden upon the beginner. However, for ambitious readers who like to take on burdens, we highly recommend a book by Gershom Scholem called simply *Kabbalāh*, published by Dorset Press (New York). This book gives an excellent and detailed account of the various schools of Kabbalistic thought. A more reader-friendly book on the subject is our own book, *The Golden Dawn Journal, Book II: Qabalah: Theory and Magic*, which is published by Llewellyn. These books contains several chapters by different authors on the various aspects of Kabbalah.

The "Limitless Light"

The ancient Kabbalists were reluctant to assign specific characteristics to their ideal of "God," since the mere designation of such qualities to a primordial deity would have been limiting—an attempt to define the indefinable. Rather than settle for a perceptible and imperfect deity, they divested their tribal god of all preconceived notions. They concluded that God was totally beyond anything in the created (limited) universe, and therefore beyond all human understanding. And the result was the concept of the *Three Negative Veils of Existence*. These veils are called *Ain, Ain Soph,* and *Ain Soph Aur.*

Ain means "negativity," "nothing," or "not." This is the outermost veil.

Ain Soph is the "limitless." Ain Soph is the middle veil. It is the vessel that contains the Ain.

Ain Soph Aur means "the limitless light." This is the innermost veil from which our conceptions of deity and the universe were formed. Ain Soph Aur is the specific light that is the result of the junction of *Ain* and *Ain Soph*.

The concept of the *Three Negative Veils* defies human attempts to describe these veils as *something*. They are planes of existence that lie outside of all human realms of experience. Humankind naturally thinks in terms of "somethings" rather than "nothings." We simply cannot understand these veils in terms of anything we can compare them to. The student is reminded of yet another polarity of the Kabbalah—just as the light cannot exist with darkness, "something" cannot exist without "nothing." *Ain* is truly the only constant in the universe, it has always been, and will always be. "Somethings" always need a point of beginning, even the highest sphere of Kether. The *limitless nothing*, on the other hand, has always existed. All of creation springs from and returns to it. It is the calm silence, the limitless light of *being*—infinity. The unmanifest veils of negativity contain within themselves the seeds of positive existence and the manifest universe as we know it. This negativity can be symbolized by the Greek letters *alpha* and *omega*, the beginning and the end.

In spirituality it is impossible to avoid the perception that the ultimate deity is a limitless entity (or perhaps a non-entity) who encompasses everything in the universe in indistinguishable manner. But it is equally impossible to evade the idea of a preeminent creator being. The concept of the *Sephiroth* evolved to elucidate the creative process through which the perfect limitless deity gives birth to the universe of flawed finite beings, yet still retains its own purity and essence.

The Sephiroth

According to Kabbalistic tradition, the *Ain Soph* began to unfold its energy into the universe as we know it, through different stages or levels, although there was no interaction between the *Ain Soph* and the limited universe of creation. Each successive level became more dense than the previous one. This divine energy originated from nothingness, acquiring substance as it descended into the different stages of manifestation. The energy issued forth following a cyclical pattern of emanation, limitation, expansion, and overflow until at length, the energies solidified. The tenth level of emanation was the last, resulting in the physical universe as we know it.

The Hebrew Kabbalists referred the highest and most abstract ideas to the emanations of deity, which are called the *Sephiroth* (sef-eer-oth). Singularly they are called *Sephirah*, and they are ten in number. The Kabbalists agreed that there were ten because to them ten was a perfect number—one that includes every digit without repetition, and contains the total essence of all numbers. The number ten is therefore an all-embracing number. Outside of ten there exists no other such number, because what is beyond ten returns again to units. When arranged in a certain manner, the ten Sephiroth and the twenty-two paths that connect them form the Tree of Life. Together, the ten Sephiroth and the twenty-two paths comprise what is called the *Thirty-two Paths of Wisdom*.

The Tree of Life is the single most important symbol of the Kabbalah. Just a glance at its diagram will reveal it to be a system of perfect mathematics, symmetry and beauty. It is represented as ten circles or orbs known as the *Sephiroth*, a word that is said to mean "numbers," "spheres," and "emanations." Some see the Sephiroth as divine powers or vessels that contain the unwavering brilliance of the Divine, which is veiled and tinted by the progressively materialized spheres. The various stages of concealment make the substance of each sphere seem singularly unique to our limited minds, which are incapable of viewing the unveiled brilliance of God.

Other Kabbalists regard the Sephiroth as divine tools or instruments of the Divine (although not separated from the Divine like human tools are). All agree, however, that the Sephiroth express divine attributions or essences that are organized into an archetypal pattern which is the model for everything that has come into the manifest universe. They are the diverse expressions and mind-states of a single divine unity. Each Sephirah represents one specific aspect of god-energy, or a particular level of consciousness, while the paths that connect them are the routes that we can take to arrive at these different levels. The relationships implied in the Tree of Life underscore the whole of existence, and so the attributes of the Sephiroth may be found in any branch of knowledge. Although their basic definition is as the characteristics of the Divine, they can be described in terms of human experience because men and women are formed, as stated before, in the image of the Divine.

The symbol of the Tree of Life has gone through several evolutionary stages before arriving at the modern three-columned form that we use today (see Figure 1). One of the earliest of the Kabbalistic texts was called the *Sepher Yetzirah* or the "Book of Formation," which circulated in varying oral forms from around 100 B.C.E. to about 200 C.E., when it was standardized. This text describes the formation of the universe by comparing it with the creation of the twenty-two letters of the Hebrew alphabet.[3] Other classic Kabbalistic texts include the *Sepher Bahir*, the "Book of Brilliance" and the *Sepher Zohar*, the "Book of Splendor," which were published in 1180 and 1285, respectively.

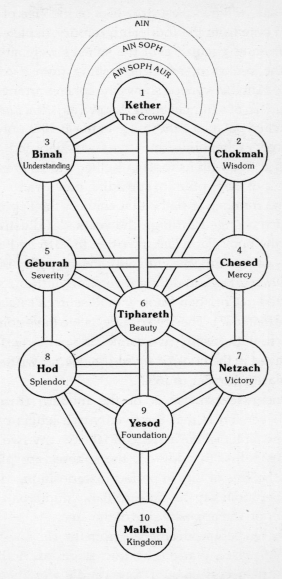

Figure 1: The Tree of Life

Some of the earliest drawings of the Tree of Life, which date from the fourteenth century, depicted the Sephiroth as circular, as if the spheres were situated like the spokes of a wheel, issuing from a central source. Another version shows the spheres arranged in the pattern of a human being, known as *Adam Kadmon*, the archetypal man—the image of the greater universe at large.[4] Oftentimes the tree was depicted as a reversed tree with its roots in Kether and its branches (the rest of the Sephiroth) spreading downwards.

The number of paths that connect the Sephiroth has also changed through the years. An illustration from the book *Porta Lucis*, written in 1516 by Paulus Ricius, shows the Tree with only sixteen paths linking the spheres. Several different versions of the Tree are depicted in Christian Knorr von Rosenroth's *Kabbalah Denudata* (1677). The Tree of Life as we have come to know it, with twenty-two connecting paths, was first portrayed in the book *Oedipus Aegyptiacus*, written by Athanasius Kircher in 1652.

One essential aspect of the modern (Kircher-based) version is that the twenty-two letters of the Hebrew alphabet are assigned to the twenty-two connecting paths. In addition, the spheres are placed upon the Tree of Life in perfect juxtaposition, so that each Sephirah on the outer pillars counterbalances another on the opposite side of the Tree.

The ten Sephiroth emanate from the *Three Negative Veils of Existence* (various abstract stages of "nothingness") in succession as if "one candle were lit from another without the emanator being diminished in any way" and in a specific order. In this analogy, the original candle is not lessened in any way, although it gives of its essence to the candles that follow. But unlike the candle, the Sephiroth are not seen as being separated from the source. They are one with the deity, yet they are also distinct from one another, and therefore they are more easily comprehended by human beings who wish to approach the Divine through prayer and meditation.

The Sephiroth are sometimes said to have emanated in an *inward* (rather than outward or downward) fashion. In this model the Tree of Life, complete with Sephiroth, is presented as a series of concentric circles, one inside the other, all within the encompassing circle of the *Ain Soph*. The entire universe was contained within God, therefore nothing was perceived as having a separate existence outside of deity. Nothing could diminish the deity's magnificence.

The first emanation from the *Ain Soph Aur* was the Sephirah of Kether, which was distinguishable from the indifferent body of the greater *Ain Soph*, but still very closely linked with it. The first Sephirah can in effect be considered the outer aspect of the *Ain Soph*. Kether is so exalted and so closely bound to the *Ain Soph* that its qualities, like those of "the limitless," are virtually indescribable to the human mind. Since Kether is the highest "something" of which we can conceive, it is the primary focus of Kabbalistic prayer and meditation. It is "God,"[5] the source of life and light and the rest of the Sephiroth.

The first three Sephiroth of Kether, Chokmah and Binah are often referred to as the three *supernals*. They exist on a higher and more abstract level than the rest of the Sephiroth. They are also separated from the lower seven spheres by a demarcation called the *abyss*. Below the abyss are the remaining Sephiroth of Chesed, Geburah, Tiphareth, Netzach, Hod, Yesod, and Malkuth.

The Sword and the Serpent

The Sephiroth are said to have been formed from the Divine by means of the *Flaming Sword* or *Lightning Bolt* cutting through the veils of negativity, instantly creating the manifest universe in a descending current of energy or a brilliant flash of light that is reminiscent of modern science's "Big Bang" theory. Thus the emblem of the Flaming Sword resembles that of a crooked bolt of lightning, forming the natural order of the Sephiroth (see Figure 2).

Once Kether was formulated, the following nine spheres were emanated, each from the one preceding it. The result was a kind of staircase formulated between the "limitless" and the manifest cosmos. This entire process of creation from nothing into something transcends the limits of space and time. And the division between each Sephirah and the one following is infinitely brief.

The symbol of the *Serpent of Wisdom* is formed by the ascending order of the twenty-two paths that connect the Sephiroth (see Figure 3). It represents the

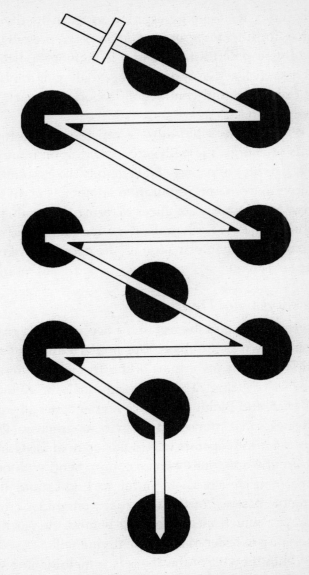

Figure 2: The Flaming Sword

reflux current of energy aspiring to reach its divine source. Together *the Sword and the Serpent* represent the two divine polarities of energy in motion—positive and negative, active and passive, exhaling and inhaling, expansion and contraction, action and reaction, cause and effect.

Whereas the Sephiroth are considered objective points of energy, the paths are looked upon more as subjective rites of passage that embody the experience of moving from one Sephirah to another. The divine energy momentarily stabilizes to form a Sephirah, yet continues to flow forth in the dynamic energy rush of the paths. (More information on the paths is given in Chapter Three.)

The Abyss and Daath

Between Binah and the rest of the Sephiroth is a great chasm known as the abyss. This marks a distinct separation from the lower part of the Tree—a difference in levels of being. The three supernals of Kether, Chokmah and Binah symbolize higher states of consciousness that transcend human awareness. The lower Sephiroth operate within the realm of ideas and thus are the only ones we can comprehend with our normal consciousness. In order to understand the intangible essence of the supernals, one must cross the abyss, which means leaving behind the earthly personality in order to reach the divine self.

Within the gulf of the abyss is something known as the "invisible" Sephirah of Daath. This is not a true Sephirah, but can be likened to a passageway across

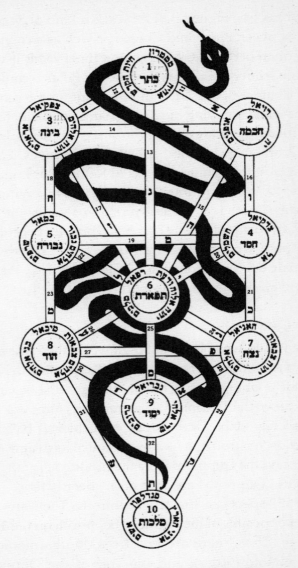

Figure 3: The Serpent of Wisdom

the abyss (see Figure 4). It serves as a kind of a mediator between Binah and Chesed as well as a conjunction point between Chokmah and Binah. This is why certain exercises such as the Middle Pillar technique (see Chapter Six) use Daath as a point on the central pillar while applying the divine names of Binah to it.[6]

Today there are some who place more emphasis on Daath than on the Sephiroth themselves. Some consider it the manifest aspect of Kether. But Daath is rather a "non-Sephirah." In many ways, trying to describe Daath is as futile as trying to describe the *Ain Soph*. In some traditions Daath is a hole that occupies the space where a Sephirah used to be, before the Kabbalistic "Fall from the Garden of Eden" which separated the supernals from the rest of the Tree.[7]

The Qlippoth

How would we know what light was if there were no darkness? Or order if not for chaos? According to Kabbalistic teachings, when the divine light first began to flow down the Tree into the Sephiroth, its force was not completely stable. It had not yet achieved balance, direction, or structure. As a result, imbalance came into being and the Qlippoth[8] were the result.

The Qlippoth are adverse, destructive, and chaotic aspects of the ten Sephiroth. They are the direct opposites of the balanced Sephiroth on the Tree of Life. Thus, there are two trees, the harmonious Tree of Life (order), and the Tree of the Qlippoth (chaos), which is said to be below the Tree of Life.

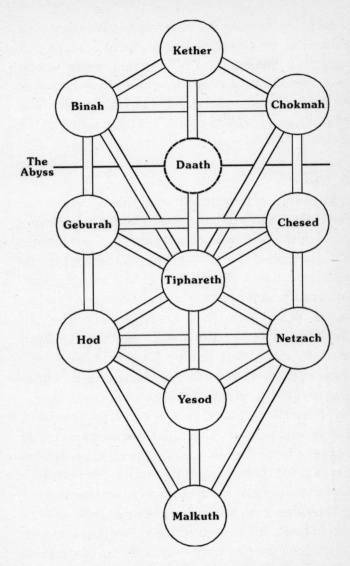

Figure 4: The Tree with Daath

For each Sephirah on the harmonious Tree there is a positive and balanced virtue. But there is also a corresponding vice which is represented by the unbalanced Qlippah on the adverse Tree. Knowledge of both the balanced and the unbalanced aspects of the Sephiroth are crucial to proper understanding of the Kabbalah.

The Pillars

The most important configuration that occurs on the Tree is that of three pillars, formed by the natural succession of the Sephiroth (see Figure 5). The left-hand pillar, also called the *pillar of severity*, consists of the spheres of Binah, Geburah, and Hod. The right-hand pillar, known as the *pillar of mercy*, is comprised of the spheres of Chokmah, Chesed, and Netzach. The central spheres of Kether, Tiphareth, Yesod, and Malkuth form the Middle Pillar, or the *pillar of mildness*.

The right-hand or white pillar is described as masculine, positive, and active. It is also known as the *pillar of force*. The left-hand or black pillar is feminine, negative, and passive. This pillar is sometimes called the *pillar of form*. The black and white pillars represent the two great contending forces in nature, and their descriptions are not meant to imply that one is good and the other evil, but rather that magnetic energy exists between these two universal opposite forces. The whole of the cosmos depends on the perfect balance of these energies.

The *Middle Pillar* is the pillar of balanced forces, the equilibrium of the other two columns.

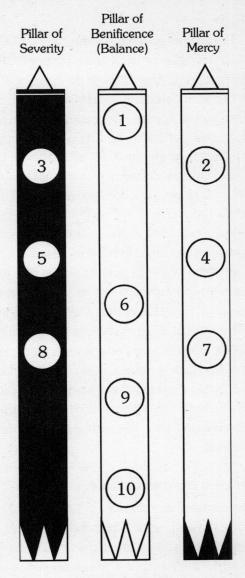

Figure 5: The Pillars

The Triads

Another important pattern on the Tree of Life is that of the three triangles or triads (see Figure 6). With this series of triangles, the Kabbalah defines the three parts of the individual *inner self* within each of us, from the supreme spiritual essence to the human ego. These triangles define three levels of *self*-consciousness. The first triangle consists of Kether, Chokmah, and Binah. This is called the *supernal triad* or the divine self. Next is Chesed, Geburah, and Tiphareth, which form the *ethical triad* or the *higher self*. Finally we have the *astral triad* or the realm of the *personality*, which contains Netzach, Hod, and Yesod.

The supernal or celestial triad is the only one whose apex points upwards to the source, the crown of Kether—the point to which the Qabalist eternally strives. The ethical triad is the seat of the higher self which seeks to unite our conscious waking self with that greater self above the abyss. The astral or mundane triad is the abode of the waking personality, normally concerned only with worldly affairs, but which can be disciplined into becoming a valuable aid for the higher self.

Sexual Polarity on the Tree

There are numerous schools of Kabbalistic thought that ascribe masculine or feminine attributes to each of the Sephiroth. Oftentimes these various sources disagree with one another. Disagreements over Kabbalah ensures that the system is kept alive, dynamic,

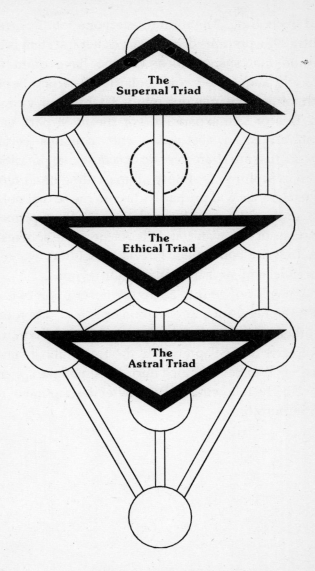

The Supernal Triad

The Ethical Triad

The Astral Triad

Figure 6: The Triads

and expanding. The minute everyone totally agrees with all the precepts of a specific esoteric system is the minute that system dies. We too have often felt strongly about the sexual polarity of certain Sephiroth, only to change our minds later as our view of the Tree of Life expanded. For the most part, each Sephirah is an abstraction that contains certain aspects that are characteristic of *both* sexual polarities. No one Sephirah is simply all masculine or all feminine. Here we will primarily discuss the sexual polarities of the spheres as they relate to the three primary elements of fire, water, and air. As far as the spheres of the Tree are concerned, Fire is masculine, water is feminine, and air is neutral or androgynous.

We will not go into a lengthy description of each Sephirah here. Such information can be readily found in other sources (see Bibliography). In addition, the Addresses of the Sephiroth in the Tree Walk, given in Chapter Two, reveal much information on the spheres as well. The following is a very brief description of the ten Sephiroth.

The Ten Sephiroth

No.	Name	Meaning
1	Kether	Crown
2	Chokmah	Wisdom
3	Binah	Understanding
4	Chesed	Mercy
5	Geburah	Severity (Power)
6	Tiphareth	Beauty
7	Netzach	Victory
8	Hod	Splendor
9	Yesod	Foundation
10	Malkuth	Kingdom

1. Kether

Kether is the first Sephirah and the highest Crown. Of all the spheres on the tree, Kether is the least dense and material. It is the first emanation out of the limitless and eternal "nothingness," and through Kether all the subsequent spheres came into being. Kether is a level of pure divine consciousness symbolized by brilliant white light. Kether is archetypally androgynous and it is the nearest concept that we can consider in terms of absolute deity—eternal God. All things in the manifest universe emanate from Kether, and to Kether all things shall return.

The number one, which encloses within itself the remaining nine digits of the decimal scale, was described by Pythagoras as the undividable monad. It cannot be divided, yet it can be defined. By the process of reflection (1 + 1 = 2, 1 + 2 = 3, etc.), the monad defines and generates all the other numbers. Kether is the starting point; it is the moment that the universe as we know it was conceived. Kether is the initial spark or first breath of the Divine. This androgynous sphere is placed at the summit of the central pillar on the Tree of Life, at the apex of equilibrium.

The *Sepher Yetzirah* says of Kether:

> *The First Path is called Admirable or Hidden Intelligence (the Highest Crown), for it is the light-giving power of comprehension of that first principle which has no beginning; and it is the Primal Glory, for no created being can attain to its essence.*

The words *Hidden Intelligence* imply a hint of the unmanifest nature of Kether. The purest seeds of life (the divine spark) are found only at the level of the first emanation, where they have always been—removed from the concept of having a "beginning point." The divine life-essence, as it descends the Tree of Life, is merely undergoing a process of transformation, from one form of energy to another (as explained in the teachings of alchemy). *The Sepher Yetzirah* also indicates that no created being can hope to attain to the pure spiritual light and essence of Kether; that would be akin to an adult human being returning to the womb to become a fertilized egg. No being using a physical organism as its vehicle of consciousness can attain to the essence of Kether. However, if consciousness has been purified to the point where it transcends thought, it receives from the "Primal Glory" the power of comprehension of the first principle.

2. Chokmah

Chokmah is the second Sephirah and the sphere of divine wisdom. This is a type of wisdom that is beyond any knowledge that we humans can comprehend. The pure energy from Kether has overflowed and created another sphere, as well as a natural polarity—*two*—the reflection of the number one. Chokmah is a sphere of pure life-giving energy. It is the great stimulating force of the universe, which starts everything into motion. The zodiac, the stars, and the constellations are attributed to Chokmah.

According to the *Sepher Yetzirah:*

> *The Second Path is that of Illuminating Intelligence; it is the Crown of Creation, the Splendor of the Unity, equaling it, and it is exalted above every head, and named by the Kabbalists the Second Glory.*

Chokmah is clearly confirmed here as the essence of illumination. It is not the same as that brilliant spark of Kether that exists on a higher plane, but as wisdom—perfect knowledge and understanding that has developed as a result of the reflection of Kether into a second sphere—a mirror of the first, enabling the divine spirit to both emanate from itself and behold itself. The "Crown of Creation" indicates that Chokmah was "created" from the crown (Kether). Again we are presented with the idea that the primal spirit is not diminished in any way through the succession of the Sephiroth, "the Splendor of UNITY, *equaling* it." That "it is exalted above every head" alludes to Chokmah's high position on the Tree along with the other supernals above the abyss.

As the first Sephirah to develop polarity, Chokmah is placed at the summit of the right-hand pillar. If Kether can be described as a point, then Chokmah could be portrayed as a straight line, an extension of the point into space. The energy of Chokmah is dynamic and outpouring, for it is the great stimulator of the universe. Within Chokmah lies the first masculine (fire) expression as opposed to the androgynous expression of Kether. Whereas Kether is the calm center point of the universe, Chokmah is complete action and movement—the vital energizing element of existence. It is the archetypal positive and the great supernal Father, Abba. However, Chokmah is not simply a masculine sexual energy, but the root essence of masculine or dynamic force.

3. Binah

Binah is the third Sephirah and the sphere of divine *understanding*. Although wisdom is the quality of

Chokmah, understanding is assigned to Binah. Wisdom alludes to complete and infinite knowledge, while understanding imparts the notion of an ability to grasp the ideas that are intrinsic to wisdom. The understanding of Binah is the divine understanding of what difficulties and hardships have to teach us in life.

Binah is the feminine counterpart of Chokmah. This sphere is situated at the summit of the left-hand pillar on the Tree of Life. Binah is the supernal Mother, Aima, the great negative or female (water) force. (By negative we mean receptive in a purely scientific way, like the positive and negative parts of an atom, not as a value judgment.) Positive and negative are inseparable properties; one cannot properly function without the other. Receptivity is a feminine function and just as in the case of Chokmah (masculinity), we are referring to sexual functions in the most basic and unmanifest of concepts. Chokmah, the Sephirah of duality, by necessity overflows into a third sphere in order for another natural polarity to occur.

The *Sepher Yetzirah* states this about Binah:

> *The Third Path is the Sanctifying Intelligence, and it is the foundation of Primordial Wisdom, which is called the Creator of Faith, and its roots are AMN; and it is the parent of Faith, from which doth Faith emanate.*

Here the Yetziratic text implies that Binah is still in a hallowed or blessed state because it remains above the abyss in an unmanifest condition. Sanctification expresses the idea of that which is holy and set apart. It is given the title "Primordial Wisdom" because it is the primary source of organization at this stage of divine emanation where a distinct polarity has been defined on the Tree of Life. Binah is here referred to as the "Creator of Faith." Faith rests upon understanding, whose parent is Binah. Faith is also defined as belief and veneration, but in the light of mystical consciousness, faith can be defined as the conscious result of superconscious experience. The average personality is not aware of this faith, but is nonetheless affected and modified by it, possibly with great feeling and emotional intensity. The statement that the roots of Binah are in AMN (Amen—meaning "firm," "faithful" and "so be it") refers to Kether. This clearly indicates that although Binah issues from Chokmah, the source of ultimate faith or truth is from the crown of Kether.

Binah is the great organizer and form-builder of the universe. Binah takes the raw energy from Chokmah and begins to organize it into form. This is the sphere of patience, limitation, and time, as well as the sphere of creation. Binah is said to be the great archetypal feminine or maternal force of the universe. Saturn, the planet of time and restriction, is attributed to this Sephirah. Binah completes the triad of the supernals.

4. Chesed

Chesed is the fourth Sephirah and the sphere of mercy and love. The mercy of Chesed is divine love, peace, and justice at the highest level. It is unconditional spiritual love. Chesed bestows great abundance, joy, laughter, and the love of life as well as love for God. It also bestows growth, expansion, and prosperity. The patterns of the Tree of Life repeat themselves after the initial three spheres are formed, therefore Chesed is the same type of energy as Chokmah, but on a lower (more manifested) level. While Chokmah may be likened to an all-knowing, all-powerful father, Chesed is the benevolent, loving and protective father, who is unselfish and forgiving. One of the lessons of Chesed is that obedience to the higher is an honor, not an indignity. Jupiter, the planet of growth and increase, is assigned to this Sephirah.

The *Sepher Yetzirah* says:

> The Fourth Path is named the Cohesive or Receptacular Intelligence; and it is so called because it contains all the holy powers, and from it emanate all the spiritual virtues with the most exalted essences: they emanate one from the other by the power of the Primordial Emanation, the Highest Crown, Kether.

The term *cohesive* again refers to Chesed's capacity to gather together all the unmanifest energies (the holy powers) it has received from the supernals across the expanse of the abyss. Again these powers or emanations are not in any way diminished as they descend the Tree and continue on the path of materialization.

This is the first sphere below the abyss and the second Sephirah on the right-hand pillar. It is therefore the first sphere of our physical universe. In Chesed can be found the structural support of all that is manifested. Chesed receives the current of divine energy, which has been modified and disciplined by Binah, and gives it another influx of energy. This begins the process of materializing the abstract energies of the supernals. Chesed is the matrix upon which the archetypal ideas will later be built into tangible form.

5. Geburah

Geburah is the fifth Sephirah and the sphere of *severity* and *might*. Other titles given to this sphere are *justice* and *fear*. The severity of Geburah is the purging and purifying fire of God that burns away all that is obsolete and useless. It is a holy and cleansing fire. Geburah also has the titles of fear and justice. This sphere rules the forces of change, which destroys the old to make way for the new. The fifth Sephirah bestows great energy, force, initiative, courage, and critical judgment. Mars, the planet of war and great energy, is attributed to this sphere.

According to the *Sepher Yetzirah:*

The Fifth Path is called the Radical Intelligence, because it resembles the Unity, uniting itself to the Binah or Intelligence which emanates from the Primordial depths of Wisdom or Chokmah.

The word *radical* here implies basic or fundamental. Here the text tells us that Geburah, the Radical Intelligence, "resembles Unity" (one of the titles of Kether). Geburah's dynamic action overflowing into the world of form bears a close relationship to the overflowing force of Kether, which is the source of all manifestation. In addition, "Unity" also implies the uniting of a new and distinct polarity in the spheres of Chesed and Geburah. Geburah "unites itself with Binah" because it is the same restrictive feminine energy of Binah on a lower, more manifest level.

Geburah is without a doubt the least understood and most feared Sephirah on the Tree. However, the natural order of the universe depends on the concept of opposites in balance, thus the benevolence, mercy and form-building functions of Chesed are now equilibrated by the harsh, destructive actions of the fifth sphere. Geburah's duty is to break down the Form issued by Chesed and apply discipline in the manner of a purging Fire. Any energy that makes its way down the Tree of Life into the material world must be tested and tempered by the opposites of Mercy and Severity. It must be cleansed in the fires of Geburah. All impurities must be burned away, just as the blade of a strong sword must be tested by the fires of the metalsmith's furnace. Only in this way can the energy be fashioned as a sturdy vehicle for manifestation. Geburah is the strong arm of God, commanding respect and burning away all that is useless or outmoded. The harsh, destructive action of this sphere is absolutely vital to further evolution. The energy of Geburah is not an evil force unless its essence spills over from justice to cruelty. Geburah is essentially a conciliatory power that restricts the merciful love of Chesed. Without the powerful force of Geburah, the mercies of Chesed would deteriorate into frivolity and weakness.

6. Tiphareth

Tiphareth is the sixth Sephirah and the sphere of beauty and harmony. This is the center of balance on the Tree of Life—the place of equilibrium that connects the higher levels of the Tree with the lower levels. It is therefore an essential conduit for passing energy and information to all levels and back again. It is the sphere of mediation and reconciliation. It is also the sphere of healing, illumination, true peace, inner tranquillity, and mystical experience. Tiphareth is also the center of the so-called Christ consciousness, the mystical center of devotion and the higher self. The luminary of the Sun, the source of life and light, is assigned to Tiphareth.

The *Sepher Yetzirah* says:

The Sixth Path is called the Mediating Intelligence, because in it are multiplied the influxes of the emanations, for it causes that influence to flow into all the reservoirs of the Blessings, with which these themselves are united.

This again refers to Tiphareth's position on the central pillar, mediating between the pillars of mercy and severity. As a mediator, Tiphareth is also seen as a connecting link between higher and lower states of being (the higher self and the lower self). This sphere is a "two-way switch" that both receives the influxes of the emanations from above, and "causes that influence to flow into all the reservoirs of the blessings." Tiphareth's neutral position on the central pillar along with its androgynous nature allows the influences to combine, multiply and increase. It is the outward manifestation of the higher and subtler Sephiroth, as well as the spiritual principle behind the lower and more manifest spheres.

The spiritual experience that takes place in Tiphareth is the Vision of the Harmony of Things. This is because the higher self, or "Holy Guardian Angel," of every individual sits in Tiphareth (referring again to Tiphareth as the mirror of Kether—the divine self). The goal of all spiritual experience is the search for the light, and this is obtained by devotion to the Great Work.

7. Netzach

Netzach is the seventh Sephirah and the sphere of victory and emotion. The victory of Netzach is the realization of the beauty and life-force that the Divine has placed in all manifested things. It is the love of nature in all her aspects. The seventh sphere is the realm of the passions that drive humans to the creative arts. Netzach is the sphere where humans begin to visualize the images of the gods, as well as to feel them with the emotions. This is also the Sephirah of social consciousness and of interpersonal relationships. Venus, the planet of love, is attributed to Netzach.

The *Sepher Yetzirah* says:

> *The Seventh Path is the Occult Intelligence, because it is the Refulgent Splendor of all the Intellectual virtues which are perceived by the eyes of the intellect, and by the contemplation of faith.*

The "Occult Intelligence" obviously refers to hidden intelligence. This is something hidden deep within ourselves that we must uncover...our divine nature that is hidden from us by mundane obstacles. The "Refulgent or Brilliant Splendor of the intellectual virtues" is the Divine White Light mediated through the prism of Tiphareth, reflected into many-rayed hues (aspects of manifestation). The one light has been reduced to the many for the purpose of manifestation into form. The phrase "eyes of the intellect" alludes to the Wisdom of Chokmah at the apex of the pillar of mercy while the passage "contemplations of faith" refers to the act of devotion, the impetus behind all spiritual attainment.

Netzach is a dynamic force that inspires us and drives us. This sphere is a reflection of the fiery Geburah, but at the level of the human personality, mediated by Tiphareth, the fire becomes desire and emotion. Art, music, dance and poetry are all expressions of Netzach energy. In this sphere we find all expressions of beauty and love, but also the less understood emotions of anger and hate, because all emotions dwell here. It is for this reason that the energies of Netzach must be balanced by its opposite, Hod. The seventh Sphere is the home of the "Group Mind," the storehouse of images and symbols in all of us, which inspires the artist, the dancer, and the musician.

8. Hod

Hod is the eighth Sephirah and the sphere of splendor. The splendor of Hod is the glory of the divine intellect and the rational mind that is a gift to humanity from God. This is the level of consciousness and the logical, reasoning mind. Hod is where we learn and where we communicate with others (as well as with ourselves). The eighth sphere governs writing, trade, magic, travel, thought processes, the accumulation of knowledge, and the exchange of ideas. Mercury, the planet of communication, is assigned to this Sephirah.

According to the *Sepher Yetzirah:*

The Eighth Path is called the Absolute or Perfect Intelligence, because it is the mean of the primordial, which has no root by which it can cleave, nor rest, except in the hidden places of Gedulah, Magnificence, from which emanates its own proper essence.

It is the "Perfect Intelligence because it is the mean (median) of the primordial." This implies a position halfway between two extremes—Force and Form. Hod is also the seat of the Intellect. To borrow the terms of astrology, this correlates to the idea of Intellect being in the house of its "dignity"—a placement that is advantageous, or "perfect." Hod's root, from which it cannot be separated, is the watery sphere of Chesed, also called Gedulah.

Hod is a lower form of the energy found in Chesed, but mediated through Tiphareth. The energy of Hod is watery (feminine) and fluidic. Hod and Netzach cannot truly function properly individually. The eighth Sphere is where the emotions and instincts of Netzach take form and come into action. Intellect needs the balance of emotion to drive it, otherwise the words and science of Hod become mere rational labelings, dead and uninspired. Likewise, emotions need the discipline of intellect to stabilize and ground, to keep the dynamic energy from being squandered. The relationship between Hod and Netzach is symbiotic. In terms of the individual, the two spheres must be in harmony and balance in order to maintain a healthy personality.

9. Yesod

Yesod is the ninth Sephirah and the sphere of the foundation. By foundation, we mean the astral foundation or matrix where all manifested forms in the physical universe are based and built on. It is the sphere of the astral place and the level at which we can build up images in the imagination. Yesod touches upon the images and operations of the unconscious mind—those subconscious body functions that we are unaware of. The ninth sphere is also the realm of procreation, biology, intuition, and rhythms, tides, and fluctuations. The luminary of the Moon, the ruler of the instinctive mind, is attributed here.

According to *the Sepher Yetzirah*:

> *The Ninth Path is the Pure Intelligence, so called because it purifies the Numerations, it proves and corrects the designing of their representation, and disposes their unity with which they are combined without diminution or division.*

The text states clearly that it is Yesod's duty to purify and correct the emanations. Although the emanations that flow down the Tree are intrinsically pure, they may need to be proven or corrected in order to fit them into a vehicle of dense matter. Yesod also disposes (orders) the unity of these emanations, so that only the most worthy manifested vehicles are designed for the reception of the divine energy, which is brought into the physical universe without becoming diminished in any way from its essential purity.

The spiritual experience of Yesod is the Vision of the Machinery of the Universe. What this implies is that Yesod is the sphere of the astral light, also known as the *akasha*. This is the etheric substance that underlies all dense matter. It is the astral matrix upon which the physical universe is built. Yesod is the receptacle of influences from all of the preceding Sephiroth...which are then combined into a type of blueprint made from the astral light. This blueprint is the "foundation" or etheric double where the earthly plane is constructed. All events, whether natural or humanmade, occur in the aethers of Yesod *before* they occur in the physical world. The ninth Sephirah is that final step that activates the last manifestation of form. In the same manner, all the Planets were born out of the mind of God, and all humanmade inventions first appear as ideas in the Yesodic part of the inventor's mind. Yesod is the seat of intuition in humankind. In addition all magical operations take place in the sphere of Yesod, because the magician seeks to effect changes in the physical world by manipulating the subtle currents of the astral.

10. Malkuth

Malkuth is the tenth and final Sephirah and the most dense and material of all the spheres. It is known as the kingdom, because it alludes to the physical universe in which we humans exist. Malkuth is the corporeal cosmos as we know it. The tenth sphere is the closest to our normal waking consciousness. It is the earth, the air, the ocean, and the solar system. It is the divine clothed in matter. It is granite, wood, sand, and flesh. This is this level of divinity that has the most immediate influence on our material and physical circumstances. The planet earth is assigned to this sphere.

According to the *Sepher Yetzirah*:

> *The Tenth Path is the Resplendent Intelligence, so called because it is exalted above every head, and sits on the throne of Binah. It illuminates the splendor of all the Lights, and causes an influence to emanate from the Prince of Countenances, the Angel of Kether.*

The title "Resplendent Intelligence" implies a close relationship between Malkuth and Kether, the first and last sphere of the Tree. At this point the emanations are completed and the result is the brilliance of the unified Tree of Life. Malkuth now becomes Kether of another Tree on another level. The mention of the throne of Binah implies another close relationship: Binah, the great mother, is the primordial giver of form, while Malkuth, the lesser mother, is the final giver of form.

Malkuth is the only sphere that has achieved stability and inertia (a period of rest). It is also the only sphere that is not a part of a triad. The tenth and final sphere receives the etheric framework of manifestation (the influences from Yesod) and completes the building process by grounding the energy in matter. Malkuth is the container for the emanations of the other nine Sephiroth.

Another title of this sphere is "the gate," which implies that we as physical beings live out our lives in the realm of Malkuth, only to pass through the gate upon leaving our bodies behind.

There is an abundance of different associations that are attributed to the Sephiroth. Only through meditation and study will some of these correspondences become clear. But some of the major ones will be briefly explained here. Each Sephirah has a descriptive Hebrew *name* by which it is known and a powerful *divine name* that represents the specific god-aspect that resides at that level. The divine name of a Sephirah is by far the most important and holy of all associations belonging to that sphere. There are also *archangelic* and *angelic* names that refer to the celestial inhabitants of the sphere. These beings are our teachers and guides on the path to spiritual evolution, residing as they do in the realms between God and human. A host of lesser associations, such as gemstones, plants, scents, etc., are useful additions designed to stimulate thought and focus.

By studying, meditating upon, and working with the Kabbalistic Tree of Life, we are striving to increase our perceptions and become conscious of the powers and energies that have parallel existence within the greater universe of deity and the lesser universe of humanity—*ourselves.* By using Kabbalah in our daily lives, we become as living Trees of Life, with the potential to connect with every facet of the divine powers of the cosmos.

Endnotes

1. From Eliphas Levi's *The Book of Splendours*, page 127.

2. For an example of this see the article called "She Dances on the Tree" by Oz in *The Golden Dawn Journal, Book II: Qabalah: Theory and Magic.* In this article the author presents a Kabbalistic Tree of Life that is composed only of Goddesses.

3. The *Sepher Yetzirah* in its modern form includes an appendix section called "The Thirty-Two paths of Wisdom," which refers to the ten Sephiroth and the Twenty-two connecting paths. Passages from this tract are quoted often in this present book to help clarify the characteristics of the Sephiroth and the paths. The term *Yetzratic Title* indicates a designation given to a particular path by the *Sepher Yetzirah.*

4. This glyph is also important in the application of Sephirotic ideas and energies to the human being—the lesser universe. See Chapter Four for more on this.

5. We use the uppercase *God* not because of the Judaeo-Christian penchant for asserting the superiority of their god over all others, but rather when the term is used to describe the totality of existance. This concept of "God" includes all the gods and goddesses, who are specialized aspects of "God."

6. If Daath can indeed be described as a tunnel leading across the abyss, then the first Sephirah one would see looking up through the tunnel would be Binah.

7. For more information on the Garden of Eden as it applies to Hermetic work, see pages 367–371 and pages 554–556 in our book *Self-Initiation into the Golden Dawn Tradition*.

8. The singular form is "Qlippah."

CHAPTER TWO

THE TREE WALK

The Tree of Life can be experienced in a variety of different ways that will help facilitate spiritual health, growth, and awareness. One way is to visualize the spheres as they exist within the human body using what is called the *Middle Pillar Exercise.* Another method is through daily affirmation and prayer. But perhaps the most effective tool for swift comprehension of the Sephiroth is a ritual drama called *Walking the Tree of Life* or simply *"the Tree Walk."*

Learning Kabbalah through Ritual Drama

Ritual drama has been used throughout the ages as a device for teaching spiritual truths, religious mythologies, and cultural legends. In ancient Sumer, the *hieros gamos* or holy marriage between the deities Inanna and Dumuzi was reenacted annually as a celebration that also served to instruct the people to respect the cycles and fecundity of nature. The Graeco-Egyptian mystery religions often involved the reenactment of certain divine death-and-resurrection myths of various deities—including Dionysos, Mithras, Isis and Osiris, Demeter and Persephone, and Attis and Cybele. In modern times, Christian myths are staged in passion plays, while Wiccans dramatize the death-and-rebirth cycles of the Oak King and the Holly King from European folklore.

The Kabbalah, too, can be ritualized in the time-honored tradition of ceremonial drama. *The Tree Walk* is but one form of ritual drama that can be used to illustrate Kabbalistic principles in a vivid manner.

What Is a "Tree Walk?"

People who have little understanding of the Kabbalah often approach the subject as if it were a dissertation for a doctoral degree in quantum physics. Indeed, the Kabbalah presents itself as a mystical system that is based on numbers and abstract ideas. This sometimes makes it a difficult system for "left-brained" and experience-oriented individuals to grasp. The most ancient Kabbalistic texts do not help to facilitate understanding either, oftentimes using riddles and arcane symbolism to illustrate spiritual truths. Many times we have been approached by students who tell us, "I'd like to study Kabbalah, but the Hebrew words put me off," or "it's a patriarchal system," or "shamanism and Neo-paganism are more my path because Kabbalah is all theory and book work."

We are all too aware of the problems some individuals have in understanding the Kabbalah. But such difficulties need not exist. The Kabbalah can be *experienced* just as any other mythos—using the tools of drama, humor, song, and poetry. The basic tenets of Kabbalah can be easily understood by anyone, by bringing the system to life in what we have come to call *Walking the Tree of Life*. The *Tree Walk* can be described as performance art, a theatrical piece, or a ritual drama. Regardless of how one describes what the Tree Walk is, *what it does* is infinitely more important. By representing the Sephiroth of the Tree of Life with living, thinking, and feeling human beings, these abstractions are suddenly brought into sharp focus in a profound way that cannot be duplicated. Years of studying Kabbalistic books cannot compare with the perceptions that are gained through experiencing the Tree in this fashion. Even individuals who have had no contact with Kabbalistic teachings whatsoever will come away from this event with a great deal more understanding of the subject.

We hope to provide readers with a method for learning and teaching Kabbalistic principles in a way that is informative as well as entertaining. We also hope that *Walking the Tree of Life* emerges as a tradition of its own, and that this Kabbalistic ritual drama is performed by people from many different spiritual paths who wish to apperceive the mysteries of the Kabbalah on a personal level that they can easily relate to in their daily lives.

What Happens in the Tree Walk

As in any piece of performance art, the players must be chosen to play the roles assigned to them. In the Tree Walk, ten people are chosen to represent the ten Sephiroth on the Tree of Life. They wear appropriately colored robes and insignia, and they are usually surrounded by symbols that represent their stations. The "stage" the "players" perform on should be a very large room—large enough for the players to space themselves out evenly in the Tree of Life formation, with plenty of room between each station. (If a large room is not available, different pairs of Sephiroth can be stationed in separate rooms.)[1]

One additional person is chosen to act as the *Hermit* or primary guide on the Tree of Life. The Hermit may wear a nondescript robe and/or headdress and walk with a staff, or be dressed informally. It is the Hermit's duty to lead all the participants (known as the *Tree Walkers*) from Sephirah to Sephirah. The Tree Walkers are brought into the room by the Hermit who guides them to each station from

Malkuth to Kether, following the progression of numbered Sephiroth backwards from ten to one—from the physical world of humanity back to the godhead. The "players" or *Sephirotic guides* represent the spheres on the Tree. Each one has a speech or scripted address that they recite to the Tree Walkers. The Tree Walkers, led by the Hermit, move as a group to each station, until at length they reach the first Sephirah of Kether. From the second sphere of Chokmah the Tree Walkers are led individually into Kether.

The Sephirotic guides may remain at their stations until the Tree Walk is completed, or they may choose to join in the procession once they have finished with their dialogue. The Tree Walk is concluded once all participants have entered the station of Kether.

As an alternative, the Tree Walk could be presented on an actual stage, using a curtain to separate the scenes. The "acts" of the play could also be divided by dimming the lights between each scene. In this instance only one or two people would be needed to play all the parts.

The History of the Tree Walk

We can't say for certain when and where the Tree Walk as a concept first originated. Our group has been performing different variations of it since 1988. And we've heard of other groups performing something like it for about as long. Suffice it to say that the *idea* of the Tree Walk has occurred to several Kabbalistic-minded individuals over the last few years.

The Tree Walk, as we know it, has undergone some changes, but has essentially remained the same. Sometimes certain stations or Sephiroth on the Tree of Life were represented by individuals, while at other times they were represented by objects. (For example: In some of our earliest Tree Walks, Malkuth was symbolized by an area or darkness, illuminated only with a harsh strobe light. A beach ball covered with a map of the Earth served as the sphere of Malkuth, which was bounced back and forth by the participants.) Sometimes, the so-called "invisible Sephirah" of Daath was represented by a person, at other times not. There was no scripted dialogue in the early days, so each person representing a Sephirah had to perform their roles in an improvised manner, although they had to have a thorough grounding in Kabbalisitc knowledge beforehand.

Variations on the Tree Walk are always possible. Some groups may wish to include actors dressed up as the unbalanced forces of the Qlippoth, who would appear at certain intervals to mock the audience, tempt the participants off the ascending paths up the Tree, or even taunt the Hermit—only to be put in their place by the Sephirotic guides.

Today, our group performs the Tree Walk regularly using the scripted dialogue that we have provided in this book. But even if the words are always the same, each performance of the Tree Walk is different, as new participants are recruited to play the roles of the various Sephiroth, bringing their own unique perceptions and talents to bear on the event.

Improvisation

Although the basic speeches of the Sephirotic guides are provided in this book, there certainly is (and should be) room for improvisation. Personal experience, creativity, and impromptu dialogue should be welcomed and encouraged. All of these things will only serve to make the Tree Walk more fresh and innovative.

A natural polarity exists between certain pairings of Sephiroth on the Tree of Life (especially Malkuth and Yesod, Hod and Netzach, Geburah and Chesed, and Binah and Chokmah). This pairing of energies easily lends itself for spontaneous dialogue between the Sephirotic guides. At times this type of ad-libbing can be quite entertaining. For example: Yesod can chide Malkuth about working too hard and focusing on the material. Likewise, Malkuth can lecture Yesod about not being grounded and having his/her head in the clouds. Hod can admonish Netzach about being too emotional and impulsive, and in return, Netzach can tease Hod about being a bookworm who needs to get out and play more. Geburah threatens the Tree Walkers and Chesed consoles them. Binah and Chokmah can trade marital remarks with each other.

Of all the "players" the Hermit has the most freedom to improvise about all aspects of the Tree Walk (see Figure 7). He may ask the Tree Walkers how their journey is progressing. He might chide the Tree Walkers about being too hasty, or too slow. He may converse with all of the Sephirotic guides. He can even ask questions or make comments about the Sephiroth as each station is encountered.

If the Sephirotic guides are thoroughly grounded in Kabbalistic knowledge, they might invite the audience to ask questions, so long as they do not get bogged down in boring long-winded explanations. Remember, the object is to keep it flowing and interesting. Certain individuals could be "planted" in the audience with predetermined questions in case the audience is a bit too timid to ask.

Variations in the Tree Walk include:

1. Adding the pseudo-Sephirah of Daath. This can be done by merely indicating a circle on the floor in the position of Daath between Chesed and Binah. Or it might be played by a person veiled as a ghost.

2. Adding players or symbols to indicate the connecting paths between the Sephiroth. Dialogue and stage directions for these variations of the Tree Walk are given in Chapter Three.

Figure 7: The Hermit

How to Get Started on the Tree Walk

All participants should reread the following chapter for familiarity with the concept of the Tree Walk, especially the individual Sephirotic stations. Readers should be acquainted with the correspondences of each sphere, although they do not have to be committed to memory. The necessary symbolism (props and robes) should be obtained. If possible, the Addresses of each station should be memorized by the Sephirotic guides who are assigned those roles. (This is not a necessity, however.)

If there are not enough persons to fill all the parts, double or triple up on the various roles. The technical requirements for this could be minimal: costumes, make-up, special lightning, or even masks.

What to Expect in the Tree Walk

Expect to learn about the Kabbalah in a new and vitalizing way. Expect to laugh. Expect to cry. Expect to be entertained. Expect the unexpected. Expect to feel like you have shared something important with others. Expect to want to do it again.

CHAPTER THREE

THE SEPHIROTIC STATIONS

Malkuth

(Mahl-kooth)

Translation of Name: Kingdom

Sephirah number: Ten

Position on the Tree: At the base of the Pillar of Equilibrium (the Middle Pillar)

Keyword: Completion, stability

Usual Color: Citrine, olive, russet, and black

Divine Names: Adonai ha-Aretz (Ah-doe-nye ha-Ah-retz), *"Lord of Earth"*; Adonai Melekh (Ah-doe-nye Mel-ek), *"Lord and King"*

Archangel: Sandalphon (San-dahl-fon)

Angelic Choir: Ashim (Ah-sheem), *"Souls of Fire"*

Material World: Olam Yesodoth (Oh-lahm

Yeh-so-doth), *"World of Foundations,"* The sphere of the elements, the planet Earth

Yetziratic Title in Hebrew: Sekhel Mitnotzetz

Yetziratic Title in English: The Resplendent Intelligence

Additional Titles: The Gate, the Gate of the Garden of Eden, the Gate of Death, the Gate of Justice, the Gate of Prayer, the Gate of the Daughter of the Mighty Ones, the Inferior Mother, *Malkah,* "the Queen," *Kallah,* "the Bride," *Atarah,* "the Diadem"

Magical Image: A lovely young woman, crowned and throned

Spiritual Experience: A divine vision of the Holy Guardian Angel

Virtue: Discrimination

Vice: Avarice, Inertia

Correspondences on the Body: The feet

Tarot Cards: The four Tens, the four Princesses

Symbols: The equal-armed cross, the mystic circle, the triangle of art (evocation), the Hebrew letter Heh-final, the double-cubical altar

Scent: Dittany of Crete

Minerals: Rock crystal, salt

Plants: Oak, cypress, grains, potato, turnip, cotton, patchouli

Associated Gods: Geb, Osiris, Nephthys, Tammuz, Ceres, Pluto, Demeter, Persephone, Gaea, Nerthus, Brigid, Dana

Figure 8: The Guide of Malkuth

The Station of Malkuth

The Sephirotic guide of Malkuth in the Tree Walk may be either a man or woman. The guide should be seated to emphasize the fact that of all the spheres, Malkuth is the only one that is stable, heavy, and inert. The guide sits at the table, immersed in writing as the Tree Walkers approach. Yet there can and should be objects at the station of Malkuth that suggest the great amount of physical activity that takes place there. A variety of moving, battery-operated toys can be placed at the station for this purpose. These will not only give the impression of a hectic and bustling physical realm, they will also add a humorous touch as well.

The station of Malkuth should be perceived by the Tree Walkers as practical, businesslike, no-nonsense, and very important (see Figure 8).

Symbolism

Guide: Male or female

Robe Color: Either black or the four colors of Malkuth: citrine, olive, russet, and black

Secondary Color: White (a white headband, head-dress, belt, sash, collar, etc.)

Lamen Symbol: Either a dekangle or the number ten in white against a background of black or the four Malkuth colors

Props and Additional Symbols: A table and chair.
The four elements (a red candle, a cup of water,
a rose or incense, and a platter of salt) on the
table. A pad of writing paper and a pencil or
pen. A couple of battery-operated toys under the
table.

The Address of Malkuth

"Come on in and sit down. Welcome to the Kingdom!
Have a seat and ground yourselves. It feels good to be
grounded, doesn't it? Good old Terra Firma. I'll be
with you in just a second. I'm just finishing up these
tax forms. (Pause). There. It seems like I'm always
busy. If it's not one thing it's another. There's always
something happening here in Malkuth. Sometimes it
can be pretty distracting!

"Yeah, I get all types of people coming through
here. This is the busiest Sephirah on the whole Tree.
I've seen lots of action. But most people that come
through here are so wrapped up in the physical
world of the senses, they think that the earth plane is
all there is. They don't even know that there are nine
more spheres on the Tree to explore! They can't see
anything beyond! How sad!

"Then I get a few spiritual types that come through
here. Most of them are OK, but some of them look
down on me, like I'm not a real Sephirah like the others. Boy, that gets me mad. Don't they realize that mat-

ter is just as sacred as spirit? That both come from the creator of the universe? Matter is the bride of spirit. Malkuth is a vast temple!

"'Talk not of temples, there is one
"'Built without hands, to mankind given;
"'Its lamps are the meridian sun
"'And all the stars of heaven,
"'Its walls are the cerulean sky,
"'Its floor the earth so green and fair,
"'The dome its vast immensity,
"'All nature worships there.'"2

"This is Malkuth! A sphere that is every bit as holy as Kether. This is where the physical and the spiritual meet and blend. This is the home of the four elements of fire, water, air, and earth. All of the combined energies of the other nine Sephiroth rush down the Tree so that they can manifest here in Malkuth. So that human beings can touch the rocks and the earth and drink the cooling waters of the divine universe. So that they can literally touch the hand of God!

"But don't get me wrong, I want every one of you to explore ALL of the other spheres on the Tree. That's what it's all about. But remember, don't take Malkuth for granted! I am not called the Gate for nothing. I am the Gate of Death and the Gate of Tears. But I am also the Gate of Justice and the Gate of Prayer. I am the Gate of the Garden of Eden. I am Malkah—the Queen, and Kallah—the Bride. As long as you live in physical bodies, you remain within my Gate. Only when you are released from the physical body do you pass beyond my Gate.

"Malkuth is full of wondrous things, both sublime and lowly. Everything you can think of is here. The good, the bad, and the ugly. YOU have to learn to use your sense of discrimination here. That is the virtue of Malkuth—you must decide between right and wrong—good and bad. It's your decision. But be careful of those two great vices of Malkuth—laziness and greed for material things. Those are the things that will throw you off the spiritual path here.

"Listen closely to what I have to tell you. In order to gain true spiritual growth, you have to be able to survive right here in Malkuth first. If you can't cope with the physical world, then you have no business dabbling in the astral world. Get your house in order first. Then you can go on to explore the higher levels of the Tree. But remember that I'm here to ground and stabilize you if you get off balance.

"Also remember that the spiritual experience of Malkuth is the Vision of the Holy Guardian Angel. This is your inner self, which is hidden within the shell of the body. Here in Malkuth, you can begin to examine those hidden realities that are beneath the outer physical realities. That's really what Malkuth is all about—using your abilities to look beyond outer appearances to see the beauty of spirit within. Having the ability to see the harmony of spirit balanced with Matter.

"Well, I gotta get back to work. I've got an awful lot to do! Don't want to sit still for too long, or inertia will set in. It's been great talking with you, but I know you want to move on. But don't worry, you haven't seen the last of me. I'll be talking to you many more times throughout your lifetime. Have a pleasant journey! Farewell!"

(*Malkuth goes back to writing.*)

Yesod

(Yeh-sod)

Translation of Name: Foundation

Sephirah number: Nine

Position on the Tree: Toward the base of the Pillar of Equilibrium (the Middle Pillar)

Keyword: Astral Light

Usual Color: Violet

Divine Name: Shaddai El Chai (Shah-dye El-Chai), meaning *"Almighty Living God"*

Archangel: Gabriel (Gah-bree-ale) meaning *"the Strength of God"*

Angelic Choir: Kerubim, meaning *"the Strong Ones"*

Material World: Levannah (Leh-va-nah), Luna—the luminary of the moon

Yetziratic Title in Hebrew: Sekhel Tahur

Yetziratic Title in English: The Pure Intelligence

Additional Title: Tzaddik—"the Righteous One"

Magical Image: A beautiful naked man, very strong

Spiritual Experience: A vision of the Machinery of the Universe

Virtue: Independence

Vice: Idleness

Correspondences on the Body: The groin area and reproductive organs

Tarot Cards: The four Nines

Symbols: The perfumes and sandals

Scent: Jasmine

Minerals: Quartz

Plants: Willow, moonwart, lotus, lemon, gardenia, mushroom, poppy

Associated Gods: Shu, Sin, Khonsu, Artemis, Selene, Hecate, Sif, Varuna

The Station of Yesod

The Sephirotic guide of Yesod in the Tree Walk may be either a man or woman, although a woman may be preferred. The guide may stand, sit, kneel, or even lie flat on the floor as the Tree Walkers approach, but should also alternate these positions—even rocking back and forth or slowly dancing—to show that the sphere of Yesod is changeable, fluidic, and erratic. The guide should be covered with a violet veil to emphasize Yesod's aura of mystery (see Figure 9). A censer of incense should be burning as the guide gently moves the smoke with a hand-held fan.

Figure 9: The Guide of Yesod

69

Symbolism

Guide: Male or female (female preferred)

Robe Color: Violet (veil may also be violet)

Secondary Color: Yellow (veil, headband, headdress, belt, sash, collar, etc.)

Lamen Symbol: Either an enneangle, or the number nine in yellow against a violet background

Props and Additional Symbols: Veil, censer of incense, fan, strobe light, a crystal ball, two pillars immediately behind the guide, one black and one white

The Address of Yesod

"Who approaches the astral realm? Ah! I see a group of hardy travelers who wish to climb the Tree of Life. Is the physical world of Malkuth not enough to satisfy you? Is the material plane not enough to quench your thirst for spiritual knowledge?

"'All thought becomes an image and the soul
"'Becomes a body: that body and that soul,
"'Too perfect at the full to lie in a cradle,
"'Too lonely for the traffic of the world:
"'Body and soul cast out and cast away
"'Beyond the visible world.'"[3]

"You have entered Yesod, the foundation—the realm of the astral light. Everything that manifests into matter must be created here first. For in Yesod is the blueprint *behind* all matter. Everything has an astral body—rocks, trees, objects, animals, humans— all have an astral double that exists here. The spiritual experience of Yesod is the Vision of the Machinery of the Universe. That which is *behind* the physical.

"The etheric substance that makes up all astral forms has been called many things, including ecto-plasm and aethyr. It is the astral light or *Akasha*, a substance that is related in nature, to both mind and matter. The divine creator molds everything out of this astral substance before molding it into matter.

"This is the stuff that makes magic work. The magician can also mold and manipulate this astral light—eventually causing change to occur in the physical plane. The subtle currents of the astral are invisible to many, but those who know them may use them to alter the material plane. They may also be used to journey to the ends of the universe.

"For Yesod is the sphere of dreams, visions, pre-monitions, divination, and prophecies. It is the sphere of imagination and intuition—of knowing and seeing things that are invisible to the five senses.

"The moon is the planet attributed to Yesod. Like Luna, Yesod is a place of cycles and change—ebb and flow—dreaming and waking. And like the moon, there is a dark side to the sphere of Yesod. For Yesod is the Treasure House of Images, filled with all of the images and visions that have been created in the mind of humanity from the beginning of time. Yesod reflects those images back to humanity today.

"Yet this is also the sphere of Maya, or Illusion. For mankind has created many images in the mind, both beautiful and terrifying. This is none other than the subconscious mind of humanity—filled with ancient and forgotten things, some of which have been repressed since the childhood of the human race.

"You must learn to be careful in the astral plane. You must learn to understand and appreciate the difference between a helpful psychic vision and an illusion created within the subconscious mind. Use your critical judgment and common sense. Do not accept all astral experiences at face value. Examine them. Test them. Rule out deceptions.

"A true spirit guide will never tell you to do something against your will. It will never demand flattery, worship, or anything else from you. If it does so, then it is a false spirit created in the realm of illusion. Banish it. Send it on its way.

"A true spirit guide from the higher levels of the upper astral plane will only offer you helpful advice or words of wisdom. Its duty will be to guide you and offer spiritual insights. Such a spirit will cultivate seeds of knowledge within you—to grow at your own pace.

"Those who would tread upon the astral winds of Yesod must remain grounded in Malkuth and remember the virtue of that tenth sphere—which is discrimination. For the mystic who has his feet planted firmly in the earthy soil of Malkuth will be better able to safely traverse the astral currents. He will obtain the virtue of Independence, while the traveler who shuns Malkuth will be unbalanced—breaking the link between matter and spirit. Such a person may invoke the vice of Yesod—which is idleness. These individuals become detached and unable to function in the physical world. They are adrift in the astral plane and a slave to numerous illusions and apparitions.

"I tell you now. Use the powers of Yesod with wisdom, balance, and strength. Believe in your own psychic abilities. Every one of you has these powers. Don't get discouraged if some of your visions, tarot readings, or psychic intuitions turn out to be wrong. No one is always right. That is the result of the ebb and the flow. Believe in yourself. Above all have trust in your own imagination. It is a sacred gift.

"The astral winds are shifting now. It is time to move on. Have a safe journey."

Hod
(Hohd)

Translation of Name: Splendor

Sephirah number: Eight

Position on the Tree: At the base of the Pillar of Severity (the Left-hand Pillar)

Keyword: Intellect

Usual Color: Orange

Divine Names: Elohim Tzabaoth (El-oh-heem Tzah-bah-oth), meaning *"God of Hosts"*

Archangel: Michael (Mee-kah-ale), meaning *"One who is as God"*

Angelic Choir: Beni Elohim (Ben-ee El-oh-heem), meaning *"Children of the Gods"*

Material World: Kokab (Koh-Kahb), the planet Mercury of our solar system

Yetziratic Title in Hebrew: Sekhel Shalem

Yetziratic Title in English: The Absolute or Perfect Intelligence

Additional Titles: Majesty, Glory

Magical Image: A hermaphrodite

Spiritual Experience: The vision of Splendor

Virtue: Truthfulness

Vice: Dishonesty

Correspondences on the Body: The right hip area

Figure 10: The Guide of Hod

Tarot Cards: The four Eights

Symbols: Names of Power, the Apron (Masonic)

Scent: Storax

Minerals: Opal, especially fire opal

Plants: Marjoram, fennel, mandrake, caraway, dill, pomegranate

Associated Gods: Enki, Nabu, Thoth, Seshat, Hermes, Athene, Asclepius, Odin, Mercury, Genesha

The Station of Hod

The Sephirotic guide of Hod in the Tree Walk may be either a man or woman, although a man may be preferred. The guide may be seated or standing. Around the guide should be stacks of books and other Mercurial items. The station of Hod should be perceived by the Tree Walkers as intelligent, conventional, energetic, excited, inspired, and eager to teach others (see Figure 10). As the Tree Walkers approach, the guide reads to them from a book.

Symbolism

Guide: Male or female (male preferred)

Robe Color: Orange

Secondary Color: Blue (headband, headdress, belt, sash, collar, etc.)

Lamen Symbol: Either an octangle or the number eight in blue against a background of orange

Props and Additional Symbols: A chair and table (optional), several stacks of books and writing materials, tarot decks, coins, ritual implements, a cup of water, Electronic gadgets (calculators, laptop computers, radios, etc.)

The Address of Hod

"Listen. You have to hear this." *(Hod reads the following, as if from a book.)*

"'True, without falsehood, certain and most true, that which is above is as that which is below, and that which is below is as that which is above, for the performance of the miracles of the One Thing. And as all things are from One, by the mediation of one, so all things have their birth from this One Thing by adaptation.

"'The Sun is its Father, the Moon is its Mother, the Wind carries it in its belly, its nurse is the Earth. This is the father of all perfection, or consummation of the whole world. Its power is integrating, if it be turned into earth.

"'Thou shalt separate the Earth from the Fire, the subtle from the gross, gently and with great ingenuity. It ascends from Earth to Heaven and descends again to earth, and receives the powers of the superiors and of the inferiors.

"'So thou hast the glory of the whole World; therefore let all obscurity flee before thee. This is the strong Force of all Forces, overcoming every subtlety and penetrating every solid thing. So the World was created.

"'Hence were all wonderful adaptations, of which this is the manner. Therefore am I called Hermes Trismegistus, having the three parts of the philosophy of the whole World. What I have to tell is completed, concerning the Operation of the Sun.'" (*Hod looks up.*)

"This passage is from The *Emerald Tablet*, a book of wisdom handed down to humanity by the master magician of ancient Egypt, Hermes Trismegistus—*the Thrice Great Hermes*.[4] I appreciate the legacy handed down by Hermes, the wise. For this is the sphere of Hod, *splendor*. It is the splendor of the intellect—the rational mind of humanity—the glory of human thought. Many great thinkers have blessed humanity with their genius: Aristotle, Plato, and Socrates. And in your own time, Carl Jung and Albert Einstein. The sciences of mathematics, energy production, and medicine have improved the quality of life for humankind. Education has expanded your minds and uplifted your spirits toward the contemplation of the Heavens.

"Primitive humans learned to communicate with one another, first by forming sounds which became words. Later, these words were turned into symbolic form, and thus the art of writing was born.

"Human beings were able to share consciousness with each other. Thoughts and ideas could be shared and experienced together. Objects could be described down to the smallest detail and categorized for better rational understanding.

"But beware the trickster! The virtue of Hod is truthfulness, but the corresponding vice is falsehood. Let me demonstrate:" *(Hod turns to one person and says):* "I will only tell you this one time. Whisper it to another person only once." *(Hod whispers into the person's ear):* "All things strive toward realization or perfection of their true natures. Pass it on."

(The audience passes along the whispered message. When the last person receives the message, Hod asks him.)

"Tell me now if you can, what was the message you were told?"

(The person tells him out loud. If it is the same message, Hod congratulates them): "Very good! You have repeated the communication correctly. The truth of the message remains." *(If it is a different message, Hod tells them):* "You see how easily communication may break down."

"How easily truth can be turned into falsehood, even with the best of intentions. You see the trickster is an archetype within us that knows truth from falsehood. This is the Hermes of the Greeks, or Coyote of the Native Americans. He is a teacher within you. But sometimes he must teach you by trickery, because humans can often be too stubborn to accept the truth of the inner teachings given to them at face value. Sometimes they must be led to spiritual truth as with a carrot.

"Words are not always enough to express spiritual communication. Such messages are not conveyed through the external exchange of words, but through the internal communication of symbols from the mind of God. As hard as you may try to express this experience to others, your most elegant words become as useless as lies. Your rational mind allows you direct communication with the Divine through the language of symbol, color, and number.

"Also with knowledge comes the temptation to use it against others who do not have knowledge. This is the vice of falsehood that you must guard against in Hod. Knowledge unbalanced can be very dangerous—take for example the technology of warfare. Wisdom and compassion must be ever invoked with knowledge, or else knowledge may be turned against humanity and lay waste to the planet.

"Hod is also the Sephirah where magicians learn to use the conscious mind to invent symbols and words to be used in magic. Here the magical books and grimoires were written. Through the use of the conscious mind, you can determine what symbols and words are needed to work magic in the astral currents of Yesod—and eventually to manifest your goals in Malkuth. The mind of the magician is a powerful tool for change and growth.

"You must leave me now, but take with you these words of wisdom: The ultimate reality of the universe is MIND. Know your own mind and you will know the mind of God. Farewell!"

(Hod goes back to reading his book.)

〜〜〜〜〜〜〜〜〜

Netzach
(Net-zach)

Translation of Name: Victory

Sephirah number: Seven

Position on the Tree: At the base of the Pillar of Mercy

Keyword: Emotions

Usual Color: Green

Divine Names: YHVH Tzabaoth (Yode Heh Vav Heh Tzah-bah-oth), meaning *"God of Hosts"*

Archangel: Haniel (Han-ee-ale), *"the Grace of God"*

Angelic Choir: Elohim (El-oh-heem), meaning *"Gods"*

Material World: Nogah (Noh-gah), the Planet Venus

Yetziratic Title in Hebrew: Sekhel Nisetar

Yetziratic Title in English: The Occult Intelligence

Additional Title: Lasting Endurance

Magical Image: A beautiful naked woman

Spiritual Experience: A vision of Beauty Triumphant

Virtue: Unselfishness

Vice: Lust

Correspondences on the Body: The left hip area

Tarot Cards: The four Sevens

Symbols: The lamp, the rose, the girdle

Scent: Benzoin, rose, red sandal

Minerals: Emerald

Plants: Rose, myrtle, elder, geranium, hyacinth,
   thyme, licorice
Associated Gods: Hathor, Ishtar, Aphrodite, Venue,
   Freya, Lakshmi, Ushas

The Station of Netzach

The Sephirotic guide of Netzach in the Tree Walk may
be either a man or woman, although a woman may be
preferred. The guide should stand to emphasize the
vitality of this sphere. As the Tree Walkers approach,
the guide plays a drum or other musical instrument
and softly sings the Chant of the Goddess. Flowers
and other objects of beauty should be placed in a circle around the guide. The station of Netzach should
be perceived by the Tree Walkers as fresh, innovative,
artistic, impulsive, sensual, energetic, liberal, and
fun-loving (see Figure 11).

Symbolism

Guide: Male or female (female preferred)

Robe Color: Green

Secondary Color: Red (headband, headdress, belt,
   sash, collar, etc.)

Lamen Symbol: Either a heptangle or the number
   seven in red against a background of green

Figure 11: The Guide of Netzach

Props and Additional Symbols: Flowers, drums, sistrums, or other musical instruments, ceramics, paintings, drawings, books of poetry, ballerina slippers, jewelry

The Address of Netzach

(The guide sings this chant approximately three or four times as the Tree Walkers approach): "Isis, Astarte, Diana. Hecate, Demeter, Kali, Inanna.

"Welcome to my garden! Isn't it beautiful? This is Netzach, the sphere of Victory. The most vibrant place upon the entire Tree of Life! Can't you FEEl it? Life isn't ALL book-work and study! Sometimes you gotta put the book aside, shut off the computer, get up off the sofa, kick up your heels and shout I'M ALIVE, for heaven's sake! Life is about feeling and experiencing! It's about *doing* something, not just talking about it.

"This is where the artist and the musician receive inspiration from the muses. This is where the dancer learns to dance and the poet dares to dream. The gods take on forms here that are pleasing to the mind of humanity. This is where humans clothe the gods in anthropomorphic form to bring them into visual focus. To make the gods seem more tangible—less abstract and remote. The gods are given human shape so that humans can connect with them emotionally. That is part of the spiritual experience of Netzach: the Vision of Beauty Triumphant.

"For Netzach is the sphere of the emotions—the passions that motivate—that drive human beings onward: love, desire, happiness. This is why the gods and goddesses of love are especially at home here: Aphrodite, Hathor, and Venus. But there are other emotions that drive people as well: hate, jealousy, and anger. All strong emotions are felt here.

"Whether you consider these negative emotions good or bad depends on what you do with them. No emotion is either good or bad by itself. Only how you act on it makes it good or bad. If seeing an injustice makes you angry, you may take that anger and do good with it by fighting against something that is wrong. A negative emotion can be used for good if its energy is transformed constructively or used as a lesson to teach you something about yourself.

"But enough talk! Celebrate the gift of life. Rejoice in the presence of the immortal Gods! Invoke often! Inflame thyself with prayer! *(Netzach recites the following discourse[5] to the Tree Walkers.)*

"'I was sent forth from the power,

"'and I have come to those who reflect upon me,

"'and I have been found among those who seek after me,

"'Look upon me, you who reflect upon me,

"'and you hearers, hear me.

"'You who are waiting for me, take me to yourselves.

"'And do not banish me from your sight.

"'Do not be ignorant of me anywhere or any time.

"'Be on your guard!

"'For I am the first and I am the last.

"'I am the honored one and the scorned one.

"'I am the whore and the holy one.

"'I am the wife and the virgin.

"'I am the mother and the daughter.

"'I am strength and I am fear.

"'I am war and peace.

"'I am senseless and I am wise.

"'I am lust in outward appearance,

"'and interior self-control exists within me.

"'Hear me, you hearers,

"'I am a mute who does not speak,

"'and great is my multitude of words.

"'I am the name of the sound,

"'and the sound of the name.

"'I am the knowledge of my name.

"' am the one who is called Truth.

"'And I am the utterance of my name.'"

(*A brief pause. Then Netzach leads audience in the Goddess chant. Slowly she leads them in a circle dance.*) "Sing with me! Isis, Astarte, Diana. Hecate, Demeter, Kali, Inanna."

"There's nothing like a good chant to warm the blood. Isn't this better than sitting around and reading all the time? I love to give my counterpart HOD over there a hard time. We're just so different! I love to tease him!

"But I must be honest with you. I really need Hod, I don't know what I'd do without him. The energies of Netzach are meant to be shared—that is the virtue of this sphere—unselfishness. But if emotions are abused to excess, the emotional love of Netzach turns into selfish lust. Do not let the copper of Venus corrode into this vice. Do not degrade my Garden of Delights. Seek ever a healthy state of balance.

"For emotion must always be balanced with intellect. Feeling must be tempered by reason. Without feeling, the intellect of Hod can become merely dead rationalizations that are out of touch with real life. But without intellect, the vitalizing energy of Netzach can be wasted—squandered away without intelligent purpose. Therefore I am tied to my brother Hod as with a loving chain. I need him to keep the mind of God and of humanity on a perfect balance.

"Ah, but BALANCE is the key! Therefore I must bid you farewell, for your journey into Netzach is at an end. As beautiful as my garden may be, you are headed for a place that is even more beautiful than this. Farewell!" *(The guide continues to chant and drum.)*

Tiphareth
(Teh-fair-eth)

Translation of Name: Beauty

Sephirah number: Six

Position on the Tree: At the center of the Pillar of Equilibrium (the Middle Pillar)

Keyword: Mediator

Usual Color: Yellow

Divine Names: YHVH Eloah ve-Daath (Yode Heh Vav Heh El-oh-ah Veh-Dah-ath), meaning *"Lord God of Knowledge"*

Archangel: Raphael (Rah-fay-ale), meaning *"the Healer of God"*

Angelic Choir: Melekim (Mel-eh-keem) or *"Kings"*

Material World: Shemesh (Sheh-mesh), Sol—the sun

Yetziratic Title in Hebrew: Sekhel Shepha Nivdal

Yetziratic Title in English: The Mediating Intelligence

Additional Titles: The Throne of Glory, Adam, the Son, *Zoar Anpin* or *Microprosopus*—the Lesser Countenance, *Melekh*—the King, the Man, *Rahamin*—Compassion

Magical Image: There are three: a majestic king, a child, or a sacrificed god

Spiritual Experience: The vision of the harmony of things. The Mysteries of the Crucifixion

Figure 12: The Guide of Tiphareth

Virtue: Devotion to the Great Work

Vice: Pride

Correspondences on the Body: The heart area, the breast, or upper part of the torso

Tarot Cards: The four Sixes, the four Princes

Symbols: The Calvary Cross, the Rose Cross, the Lamen, the truncated pyramid, the cube, the Hebrew letter Vav

Scent: Olibanum

Minerals: Topaz, yellow diamond

Plants: Sunflower, acacia, bay, marigold, saffron, rowan, peony

Associated Gods: Ra, Osiris, Apollo, Helios, Sol, Shamesh, Vishnu

The Station of Tiphareth

The Sephirotic guide of Tiphareth in the Tree Walk may be either a man or woman. The guide should be seated and relaxed to show the tranquil and balanced nature of this sphere. A chair may be used, or the guide can simply sit in the lotus position on a rug, blanket, or piece of cloth. As the Tree Walkers approach, the guide sits with eyes closed in meditation—possibly chanting "Ohm." The station of Tiphareth should be perceived by the Tree Walkers as calm, composed, and spiritually adept (see Figure 12).

Symbolism

Guide: Male or female

Robe Color: Yellow

Secondary Color: Violet (headband, headdress, belt, sash, collar, etc.)

Lamen Symbol: Either a hexangle or the number six in violet against a background of yellow

Props and Additional Symbols: A chair, a rug, a bowl of grapes, a yellow candle, a Tibetan bell, a censer of incense

The Address of Tiphareth

"Come sit down. You have come halfway up the Tree of Life and you deserve a rest. Be comfortable. Be seated." *(Tree Walkers sit.)*

"You have reached Tiphareth, the sphere of beauty. This is the center of the Tree of Life and the center of the harmony of the universe. Without balance there is chaos. Balance and harmony are what keep the fabric of the universe from tearing apart.

"I maintain the equilibrium between the Black Pillar of Severity and the White Pillar of Mercy. I am the child between these two great opposing forces. I am the mediator between them.

"The flaming fire and the torrent of water. I am the reconciler between them. The whirling air and the stable earth. I am the reconciler between them. The immortal Spirit, and the finite Matter. I am the reconciler between them.

"I am the child and I am the king. From the heights of Kether, I am as a small child gazing upward. From my position in Tiphareth, I appear like a great king to those in Malkuth. I am as innocent as a newborn child, but with the wisdom of a king.

"This is Tiphareth, the sphere of illumination and visionary sight. The monks, spiritual teachers and mystics may aspire for a lifetime to reach this position of balance and peace. This is the Sephirah of Christ-consciousness. Of Buddha-consciousness. Of Osiris-consciousness. All of the dying and resurrected gods and goddesses are at home here. Gods that were once said to be mortal, to have died and were reborn into greater spiritual glory.

"This is what is needed for anyone to truly reach the sphere of Tiphareth. The petty wants and desires of the ego, the lower self, must be sacrificed unto the higher. To the ego, which is no longer allowed to have its way, this is indeed a form of death. But to the higher self, which is then allowed to blossom like a rose, this is a rebirth, a blissful reunion.

"Then, and only then are all parts of the self awakened. The higher self in Tiphareth is free to communicate with the divine self in Kether. And it is also able to bring this illumination down into the consciousness of the lower self—which until now, did not know of its existence. A clear and open channel of divine light. It is the full recognition of the fact that human beings are spirits clothed in flesh. We are the children of the divine Creator who wished to behold himself created in matter. This is the Christ-consciousness.

"Tiphareth awakens a sense of devotion to the Spiritual. Devotion to the Great Work of ultimate union with the divine Creator. This may take several lifetimes to accomplish, but the knowledge that is learned in this lifetime will be passed along to the next. And in the next incarnation, more knowledge may be absorbed.

"But beware of the vice of Tiphareth, which is spiritual pride. The powers of Tiphareth can bring you many great and wonderful things—but always maintain an attitude of humility. Receiving a gift from Tiphareth does not make you better than any other person. And remember that gifts not cherished and cared for may easily be lost or taken away.

"I would like to give you such a gift now. I will teach you a chant that will help bring you balance. It is a threefold chant that celebrates the powers of Tiphareth. The three sounds IAO (ee-ah-oh) are symbolic of the never-ending cycle of the universe: life, death, and rebirth. It is the universal ebb and flow of life."

(Tiphareth tells the audience to close their eyes and hold hands. He then leads them in several rounds of the chant "IAO." Then Tiphareth says the following invocation.)

"'Who should not praise Thee, then, O Lord of the Universe, unto whom there is none alike? Whose dwelling is in heaven, and in every virtuous and God-fearing heart. O God, Thou vast One, Thou art in all things. O Nature, Thou Self from Nothing—for what else can I call Thee? In myself I am Nothing. In Thee I am Self, and exist in Thy Selfhood from eternity. Live Thou in me, and bring me unto That Self which is in Thee. Amen.'"[6]

When finished, Tiphareth makes a cross over the bowl of grapes, which is then passed around. Each persons takes one to eat.)

"Tiphareth is also the sphere of healing. May these simple grapes, which I have blessed with the sign of balance, nourish and maintain your physical health, as well as your mental and psychic health. May they bring you harmony and peace.

"May they also give you strength to continue your journey up the Tree. You may well need it, for a difficult Sephirah is yet to come. Remember the chant you have just learned, for it may aid you in the sphere of Geburah. Have courage and remember that your sense of balance on the Tree will see you through. Farewell!"

(The guide of Tiphareth continues meditating.)

Geburah

(Geh-boo-rah)

Translation of Name: Severity, power

Sephirah number: Five

Position on the Tree: At the center of the Pillar of Severity (the Left-hand Pillar)

Keyword: Energy

Usual Color: Red

Divine Names: Elohim Gibor (El-oh-heem Geh-boor), meaning *"Mighty God of Battles"*.

Archangel: Khamael (Kah-mah-ale), meaning *"the Severity of God"*

Angelic Choir: Seraphim (Sara-feem), meaning *"Flaming Ones"* or *"Fiery Serpents"*

Material World: Madim (Mah-deem), the planet Mars of our solar system

Yetziratic Title in Hebrew: Sekhel Nesharash

Yetziratic Title in English: The Radical Intelligence

Additional Titles: Din—"Judgment," *Pachad*—"Fear"

Magical Image: A mighty warrior in his chariot

Spiritual Experience: The vision of Power

Virtue: Energy, Courage

Vice: Cruelty, Destruction

Correspondences on the Body: The right shoulder and the right arm

Tarot Cards: The four Fives

Symbols: The sword, the spear, the scourge, the chain, the Tudor Rose of five petals

Scent: Tobacco

Minerals: Ruby

Plants: Pine, wormwood, ginger, nettle, thistle, basil, radish, pepper, holly

Associated Gods: Ninurta, Nergal, Horus, Sekhet, Mont, Ares, Mars, Thor, Agni, Durga

The Station of Geburah

The Sephirotic guide of Geburah in the Tree Walk may be either a man or woman. The guide should stand in a threatening position with a sword or spear. The guide may choose to wear a mask (or not), so long as eye contact with the Tree Walkers is possible. The station of Geburah should be perceived by the Tree Walkers as harsh and exacting, with a solid adherence to duty—yet also very caring and protective (see Figure 13).

Symbolism

Guide: Male or female

Robe Color: Red

Secondary Color: Green (headband, headdress, belt, sash, collar, etc.)

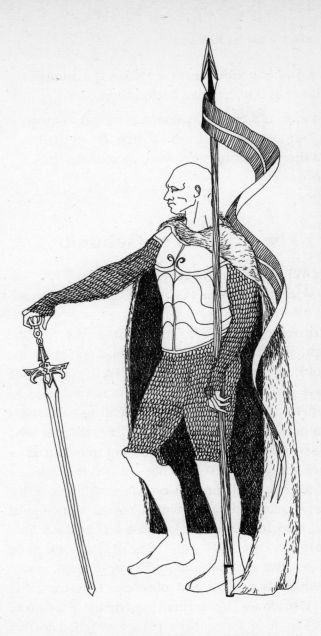

Figure 13: The Guide of Geburah

Lamen Symbol: Either a pentangle or the number five in green against a background of red

Props and Additional Symbols: A sword, a spear, a helmet, a mask, armor, a cape, chain mail, military paraphernalia such as medals, uniforms, etc.

The Address of Geburah

"Stop! Who are you and why are you here?"

(The Hermit explains to Geburah that they are travelers on the Tree of Life.)

"Travelers, are they? On the Tree of Life? Just thought you'd waltz right in here and travel up the Tree of Life, free as birds, did you? Well, you CAN'T because you're in Geburah now, and nothing sneaks past me! I am like a ferocious watchdog—a fearless gladiator. I am the warrior of the Tree, the one who watches and makes sure that nothing unbalanced or unpure goes up the Tree or comes down the Tree.

"I have several names: *Geburah,* which is severity, power, or strength, *Din,* which means justice, and *Pachad,* which means fear. I arouse fear in the minds of those who are NOT pure of heart. I am the great equalizer, the great attitude adjuster. I break down that which is useless and obsolete. I destroy that which is profane. The spiritual experience of Geburah is the Vision of Power. The planet assigned to this sphere is Mars, named after the God of War.

"'I am the bornless Spirit with sight in my feet; I am the mighty one who possesses the immortal fire; I am the truth; I am the one who hates the fact that evil deeds are done in the world; I am the one who makes the lightning flash and the thunder roll; I am the one from whom is the shower of the Life of Earth; I am the one whose mouth ever flameth; I am the one who begets and destroys. I am the grace of eternity. The heart girt with a serpent is my name!'"[7]

"Do you fear me? As well you should! Why should I let you pass by? Why should I let your journey continue? Maybe I should cut you down where you stand! Lest the Tree be profaned by your presence.

"On the other hand, maybe you have reached some sense of balance. I will offer you a chance to prove yourselves worthy of being spared from my blade. Prove to me that you have experienced the harmony of equilibrium! With all your voices blending as one, perform for me the chant that you learned in the previous sphere of Tiphareth. Sing to me the chant of the never-ending cycles of life, death and rebirth. Prove that you have obtained balance!"

(Prompted by the Hermit, the audience chants "IAO" several times. When satisfied with their performance, Geburah holds up his hands.)

"Very well. Very well. You have proven yourselves to be worthy and balanced travelers upon the Tree of Life! And I salute you for having the courage to face me. Not many do.

"Mine is not always an enviable position. Many do not understand me at all. There are good reasons for my harsh attitude. I must do what needs to be done at all times. If an army threatens a nation with warfare, I must rise to meet the challenge and protect the innocent. If a powerful stranger threatens a human child, I must fight back with the rage of a lioness defending her cubs. If someone's leg has developed a deadly infection, I must have the courage to chop it off and save the person's life. If someone weaker than myself is starving, I must have the strength to give my food to him. If a child is careless and unruly, I must have the fortitude to discipline him, for his own sake. I am the strong hand of God. I do what must be done, for the sake of the greater good.

"It is *not always enough* to be passive and easygoing. The true name of evil is imbalance and chaos. Too much mercy is but weakness and the fading out of the will. If there were no strong hand to come to the aid of goodness in the world, then evil would multiply unchecked—eventually smothering all that is good. I will not let this happen.

"Too many people believe only in the virtues of meekness, mercy, purity, and love. What about the dynamic virtues of courage, energy, justice, and integrity? Humanity must learn to accept the virtues of the warrior knight.

"But there is a vice to be avoided in Geburah. This is the vice of cruelty and destruction. Too much severity is cruelty and the barrenness of mind. Avoid this extreme. Balanced with mercy, my sword is never unsheathed in a cause that is not just. It is a mighty tool for harvesting spiritual growth—cutting away the shell and the spoilage to leave only the finest portion of the fruit.

"I do not tolerate insincerity or waste. As long as you are honest and efficient, I have no quarrel with you.

"But I'm growing tired of talking. Too much talk is wasteful. Be on your way, quickly, before I change my mind."

Chesed
(Cheh-sed)

Translation of Name: Mercy

Sephirah number: Four

Position on the Tree: At the center of the Pillar of Mercy (the Right-hand Pillar)

Keyword: Builder

Usual Color: Blue

Divine Names: El (Eh-l), meaning *"God"*

Archangel: Tzadqiel (Tzahd-kee-ale), meaning the *"Righteousness of God"*

Angelic Choir: Chashmalim (Chash-mah-leem), *"the Shinning Ones"* or *"the Brilliant Ones"*

Material World: Tzedek (Tzeh-deck), the planet Jupiter of our solar system

Yetziratic Title in Hebrew: Sekhel Qavua

Yetziratic Title in English: The Cohesive or Receptive Intelligence

Additional Titles: Love, *Gedulah*—Greatness

Magical Image: A mighty crowned and throned king

Spiritual Experience: The Vision of Love

Virtue: Obedience

Vice: Bigotry, hypocrisy, gluttony, tyranny

Correspondences on the Body: The left shoulder and the left arm

Figure 14: The Guide of Chesed

103

Tarot Cards: The four Fours

Symbols: The pyramid, the square, the orb, the equal-armed cross, the crook, the scepter, the wand

Scent: Cedar

Minerals: Amethyst, sapphire

Plants: Hyssop, fig, sage, star anise, nutmeg, sassafras

Associated Gods: Marduk, Adad, Amon-Ra, Maat, Zeus, Poseidon, Minerva, Athene, Balder, Indra, Sarasvati

The Station of Chesed

The Sephirotic guide of Chesed in the Tree Walk may be either a man or woman, although a man may be preferred. The guide may either be seated or standing, and should wear a crown. The guide should present an aura of warmth, authority, and kindness. The station of Chesed should be perceived by the Tree Walkers as strong yet reserved, good-humored, easy-going, soft-spoken, protective, and caring (see Figure 14).

Symbolism

Guide: Male or female (male preferred)

Robe Color: Blue

Secondary Color: Orange (a white headband, head-dress, belt, sash, collar, etc.)

Lamen Symbol: Either a square or the number four in orange against a background of blue

Props and Additional Symbols: A chair (optional), a crown or similar headdress, a scepter, wooden chest filled with jewelry, coins, or other trappings of royalty, Persian rug, throw pillows

The Address of Chesed

"It's all right! Come on over here. Was Geburah mean to you? Was he scary? It's OK now. I understand—and you can tell me anything. You can't really blame Geburah, you know. His job puts him under a lot of pressure. He can't help it if he's cranky. You must forgive him.

"You're safe now in the Sephirah of Chesed, or mercy. I have another name which is *Gedulah*—love and majesty. I won't let anything uncomfortable happen to you here. I'll protect you. Chesed is the sphere of helpfulness. The planet attributed to this sphere is Jupiter, the benign and loving ruler. The spiritual experience here is the Vision of Love.

"I have ruled here for many long years. I am an old and wise king. No longer do I seek the glories of battle. Now I only seek the battles of a chess match with an old friend or a grandchild. How I love to watch the children at play—to see their innocent and simple thoughts—or the love and adoration in their eyes when they look at their king. How they make me feel young again! When you have lived as long as I have, you appreciate the goodness in the simple things of life.

"A good King or queen must rule the people with love—like a parent—governing with the heart, not the sword. Mine is a stable and orderly kingdom. I govern with mercy and justice, for the good of my subjects. Because of this they know the virtue of obedience. For when the ruler is just, it is an honor to obey his laws. Just as the mundane must eventually obey the spiritual.

"'The quality of mercy is not strained;
"'It droppeth as the gentle rain from heaven
"'Upon the place beneath: it is twice blest;
"'It blesseth him that gives and him who takes:
"''Tis mightiest in the mightiest: it becomes
"'The throned monarch better than his crown;
"'And earthly power doth then show likest God's
"'' When mercy seasons justice.'"[8]

"The vices of Chesed are the social vices of bigotry, tyranny, and gluttony. These are the result of love that has turned selfish and superficial. This is to be avoided. Love must be shared, not hoarded.

"Chesed is the sphere of exalted consciousness. It is the sphere where the highest Adepts communicate with the illuminated masters who are without physical form. Here the great spiritual teachers who have left this world still instruct those who are less evolved.

"Those living mystics who are fortunate enough to rise to the height of Chesed usually do so after a long and full life. They are ready to shake off the chains of the physical body and pass beyond the material world. To be freed from the wheel of life and death—evolved to the point where they do not need to be born again into human bodies. They may join directly with the eternal God. Or they remain in the higher planes, becoming illuminated masters themselves—disincarnate consciousness—disciplined by form, but now formless. Bodiless masters who help to clarify abstract spiritual ideas to those initiates still living on Earth.

"Like Malkuth, Chesed is a sphere of formation. That is because the position of the fourth Sephirah makes it a receptive and open vessel to the spheres above it. Chesed receives the energies of the three Supernals. It is the first manifestation of these powers below the great abyss. And my number—four—bears a relationship to the four elements that are found in the lower realm of Malkuth. Like the old saying goes, "as above, so below."

"But enough of my ramblings. Forgive me. You must be exhausted, and you still have a journey to complete. I hope that you have found my words to be useful. Before you go, I would like the opportunity to embrace each and every one of you, for coming to my sphere and touching my heart. "

(Chesed hugs all the Tree-Walkers.)

"Dear friends, thank you for sharing your time with me. Feel free to come back any time. You are always welcome here. In Chesed you will always find a place of refuge whenever you are in need. Have a pleasant journey. Farewell!"

∽∽∽∽∽∽∽∽

Binah

(Bee-nah)

Translation of Name: Understanding (Intelligence)

Sephirah number: Three

Position on the Tree: At the top of the Pillar of Severity (the Left-hand Pillar)

Keyword: Supernal Mother

Usual Color: Black

Divine Names: YHVH Elohim (Yode Heh Vav Heh El-oh-heem), meaning *"the Lord God"*

Archangel: Tzaphqiel (Tzaf-kee-ale), *"God's Beholder"*

Angelic Choir: Erelim (Eh-reh-leem), *"the Thrones"*

Material World: Shabbathai (Shah-bath-eye), the planet Saturn of our solar system

Yetziratic Title in Hebrew: Sekhel ha-Qadesh

Yetziratic Title in English: The Sanctifying Intelligence

Additional Titles: Ama—the dark sterile Mother; *Aima*—the bright fertile Mother; *Khorsia*—the Throne; *Marah*—the Great Sea

Magical Image: A mature woman, a matron

Spiritual Experience: The vision of Sorrow

Virtue: Silence

Vice: Avarice

Figure 15: The Guide of Binah

Correspondences on the Body: The right side of the
head or the right temple

Tarot Cards: The four Threes, the four Queens

Symbols: The womb, the yoni, the cup, the triangle,
the Vesica Piscis, the Hebrew letter Heh

Scent: Myrrh, civet

Minerals: Star sapphire, pearl

Plants: Ivy, yew, hemlock, nightshade, hemp,
aconite, cypress

Associated Gods: Ishtar, Ptah, Isis, Cronus, Saturnus,
Hera, Juno, Rhea, Frigga, Parvati, Kali

The Station of Binah

The Sephirotic guide of Binah in the Tree Walk should
be a woman. The guide may sit or stand. She cradles
a doll that symbolizes her child. As the Tree Walkers
approach, the guide gently hums or sings to the doll.
The guide should present an aura of maternity, guidance, and nurturing. The station of Binah should be
perceived by the Tree Walkers as reserved, discipli-
nary, loving, and all-knowing (see Figure 15).

Symbolism

Guide: Female

Robe Color: Black

Secondary Color: White (headband, headdress, belt, sash, collar, etc.)

Lamen Symbol: Either a triangle or the number three in white against a background of black

Props and Additional Symbols: A chair or rocking chair (optional), a doll wrapped in a baby blanket, a small child's toys and books, a clock, an hourglass

The Address of Binah

"*Shhhhhhhhh.* Not so loud! You'll wake the baby!

"Aren't children wonderful? Just think. Sperm meets egg, and before you know it, a miniature person is brought into the world. A portion of your energy leaves you and is transferred into a tiny little body—a smaller version of yourself. In the womb, your two spirits are joined. At birth, her spirit separates from your own. *Shhhhhhhhhh.*"

(*Binah hums a lullaby.*)

"'Golden slumbers kiss your eyes,

"'Smiles awake you when you rise.

"'Sleep, pretty wontons, do not cry,

"'And I will sing a lullaby.

"'Rock them, rock them, lullaby.'"9

"What a beautiful child! When she grows up, I'm going to teach her many things. I'll teach her about planets, and stars, and galaxies. About wind, and rain, and fire. I'll teach her patience, and understanding, and self-reliance.

"And as she grows I'll tell her all about the Great Goddess *Aima Elohim*—the fertile Mother of all, crowned with a crown of twelve stars, clothed with the sun, and standing with her feet upon the crescent moon. I will tell about how the Great Goddess gave birth to the planets and the celestial signs. And all about the eternal love of the Goddess for the God.

"And I will defend her from those who would harm her. For I sit at the head of the Pillar of Severity above Geburah. I will protect her with a ferocity and strength that you cannot imagine.

"*Shhhhhhhhh.* The virtue of Binah is Silence. If you are not silent, you cannot hear what is being said to you.

"As she matures, I will guide her through the joys and the sorrows of life. She will feel love and pain. She will marry and bear her own children. She will have obligations, and she will need discipline and organization to bear up under the weight of her responsibilities.

"*Shhhhhhhhhhhh.* She will have disappointments. She will be hard-working and stable, but she will yearn for greener pastures and the carefree days of childhood. But I will be there to comfort her, in her vision of sorrow. I will be there to quiet her cries and wipe away her tears. I will be her rock and her faith. When she looks into my loving eyes, she will see the divine Creator as Goddess the Mother. I will never leave her side.

"And from her limitations, she will learn true understanding of the nature of the universe. She will see that life is a beautiful and precious gift given by the Gods. She will understand that the sorrows of secular life are insignificant compared to the brilliance and richness that the spiritual life has to offer. Knowing this will lighten her heart and ease her pain. Her burdens will seem lighter, and she will laugh about them instead of complaining.

"And in her elderly years she will understand me much better. For the planet associated with Binah is Saturn, the planet of old age, and time, and patience. She will be the wise old crone, the medicine woman, the grandmother. All the while my comforting words will be in her ears.

"And when at last she dies, and her Spirit crosses the great abyss, she will return to me. I will take her back into myself, like a drop of rain falling into the sea. From my womb she was born and unto my womb she will return. Then she will be a part of me again.

"On that wonderful day, she will understand everything that I understand. We will walk together, she and I, on the crescent horns of the moon, clothed in the sun and crowned with a crown of twelve stars.

Together we will touch the source of the universe—the eye of God. We will never be apart again.

"*Shhhhhhhh.* Have patience. All in good time, my love.

"I must go now. My child is sleeping. Take care of your own children—including the child Spirit that dwells within each of you. *Shhhhhhhh.* Farewell. Farewell."

Chokmah
(Chohk-mah)

Translation of Name: Wisdom

Sephirah number: Two

Position on the Tree: At the top of the Pillar of Mercy

Keyword: Supernal Father

Usual Color: Gray

Divine Names: Yah (Yah), meaning *"Lord"*

Archangel: Raziel (Rah-zee-ale), *"The Herald of God"*

Angelic Choir: Ophanim (Oh-fan-eem), *"the Wheels"*

Material World: Mazloth (Mahz-loth), the Zodiac

Yetziratic Title in Hebrew: Sekhel Mazohir

Yetziratic Title in English: The Illuminating Intelligence

Additional Titles: *Ab*, or *Abba*—the Supernal Father, Tetragrammaton. Yod of Tetragrammaton

Magical Image: A bearded male figure

Spiritual Experience: A Vision of God Face to Face

Virtue: Devotion

Vice: ——

Correspondences on the Body: The left side of the head or left temple

Tarot Cards: The four Twos, the four Kings

Symbols: The straight line, the phallus, the Hebrew letter Yod, the standing stone, the tower, the rod

Scent: Musk

Minerals: star ruby, turquoise

Plants: Amaranth

Associated Gods: Thoth, Enki, Uranus, Coelus, Janus, Odin, Vishnu

The Station of Chokmah

The Sephirotic guide of Chokmah in the Tree Walk should be a man. The guide should be standing, seeming to study the sky with binoculars or a telescope as the Tree Walkers approach. The guide should present an aura of paternal concern, scientific inquiry, and wisdom gained through experience. The station of Chokmah should be perceived by the Tree Walkers as reserved, caring, and all-knowing (see Figure 16).

Symbolism

Guide: Male

Robe Color: Gray

Secondary Color: White or black (headband, headdress, belt, sash, collar, etc.)

Figure 16: The Guide of Chokmah

Lamen Symbol: Either a circle divided into four equal sections or the number two in white or black against a background of gray

Props and Additional Symbols: Binoculars or a telescope (a rolled-up piece of paper can serve to suggest a telescope), images of standing stones

The Address of Chokmah

"Do you see that? Do you see that comet streaking toward Jupiter? Absolutely stunning! And the constellations! Aquarius! Orion! And Pegasus! It's like seeing a vision of God face to face!"

"'Here is God's purpose—

"'for God, to me, it seems,

"'is a verb

"'not a noun,

"'proper or improper.'"[10]

"'Why indeed must "God" be a noun? Why not a verb—the most active and dynamic of all?'"[11]

(Turns to the audience.)

"Congratulations! You did it! You made it to the top of the Tree. There is only one sphere left for you to explore after this one. I always knew you had the ability to make it. You're intelligent, and you have the heart and the guts to go where you want to go in life. Don't let anyone push you around. They'll have to deal with me if they try. No one attacks a child of mine and gets away with it.

"But I hate it when people misunderstand me! They have given me this corrupted name of Jehovah! They have made me out to be some jealous angry god who punishes his children. Boy, that irritates me! The name is *Yod Heh Vav Heh!* And in reality, I am only one-fourth of that name. My name is *YAH* from the letter *Yod.* My partner, Binah, is *Heh,* my son is *Vav,* and my daughter is *Heh Finah.* And I love *all* my children!

"I know I haven't always been around for you as much as I would have liked to be. It seems like I have always had so much on my mind—so much to do. I guess I have always been a bit preoccupied—running all over the universe—making sure that the divine energy flows evenly down the Tree from Kether.

"You see I have a very important job to do. I have to channel all of the monumental raw energy from the divine source of the universe, and safely pass it down to the rest of the Sephiroth. It's like trying to hold on to a wild stallion in the middle of a hurricane! The divine light barely even stops here long enough to form the Sephirah of Chokmah before rushing down the tree in a flash of lightning.

"That's why sometimes I might seem so remote from you. It's not because I choose to be distant, but because I'm so close to the burning brilliance of Kether, that being too close to me could injure you.

"Remember the Greek myth of Semele, the mother of Dionysus? When she saw her divine lover, Zeus, in his god-form as the Thunderer, she was blasted and burnt. The sight was just too powerful.

Remember what Yod Heh Vav Heh said to Moses: "Thou canst not look upon my face and live."

"That's why I depend so much on your mother, Binah, the love of my life. She cares for you when I can't always be around. She takes on the burden of representing all three Supernals to humanity, because she is closer and more in touch with humans. She speaks to individual human beings, interceding in the form of the Shekinah, the Virgin Mary, the Holy Spirit, or the Great Mother Goddess. I don't know what I would do without her.

"But I *can* teach you many wondrous things. I am Wisdom, and I have seen the Creator face to face. I have seen the timeless birth of the galaxy from the veils which are beyond human understanding. I know of the eternal Logos—the word that shakes the foundation of the universe when spoken. I understand the mysteries of the origin of life—for I am the eternal spark that fertilizes the entire Tree of Life. I pass on the genetic codes of divinity into your souls.

"Well, even if I can't always be at your side every minute of the day, I am always with you in spirit. I am always watching you, taking pride in your accomplishments. I worry about you a lot too, because from my position I can understand a lot of things that you can't. And I've lived a long time and I've seen a lot. But I will not be a pushy parent. You must have the freedom to find your own way in life. I am confident that you will. Some day, after you've had a lifetime of experiences, maybe you'll understand me a little better. A wise man once said:

"'To me the sole hope of human salvation lies in teaching Man to regard hismelf as an experiment in the realization of God, to regard his hands as God's hand, his brain as God's brain, his purpose as God's purpose. He must regard God as a helpess Longing, which *longed* him into existence by its desparate need for an executive organ.'"[12]

"'Let none turn over books, or roam the stars in quest of God, who sees him not in man.'"[13]

"Just remember that I believe in you, and I trust your judgment. I love you, even if I don't always show it. Everything I do is for you. I would send enough energy to create four hundred Trees of Life in a fiery blaze of light for your sake.

"Well, I suppose you should get going now. You still have one more Sephirah to visit. Take care of yourselves and have a safe journey. I'm confident that you will. Farewell! Farewell!"

Kether

(Keh-ther or Kay-ther)

Translation of Name: Crown

Sephirah number: One

Position on the Tree: At the top of the Pillar of Equilibrium (The Middle Pillar)

Keyword: Source

Usual Color: White

Divine Names: Eheieh (Eh-heh-yay), *"I am"*

Archangel: Metatron (Meh-tah-tron)

Angelic Choir: Chayoth ha-Qadesh (Chai-oth ha-Kah-desh), meaning *"Holy Living Creatures"*

Material World: Rashith ha-Gilgalim (Ra-sheeth ha-Gil-gah-leem), meaning *"First Whirlings,"* the *Primum Mobile,* the first motion of the universe

Yetziratic Title in Hebrew: Sekhel Mopla

Yetziratic Title in English: The Admirable or Hidden Intelligence

Additional Titles: Existence of Existences, Concealed of the Concealed, Ancient of Ancients, Ancient of Days, the Primordial Point, the Point within the Circle, the Most High, *Macroprosopos*—the Vast Countenance, the White Head, the Head that is not

Magical Image: Ancient bearded king seen in profile

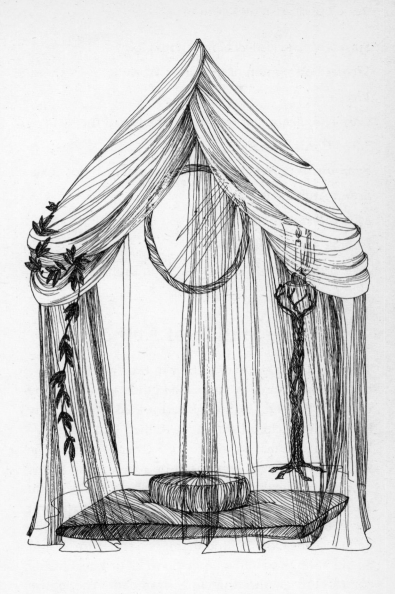

Figure 17: The Experience of Kether

123

Spiritual Experience: Union with God

Virtue: Completion of the Great Work

Vice: ———

Correspondences on the Body: The top of the head

Tarot Cards: The four Aces

Symbols: A crown, a point, a swastika or fylfot cross

Scent: Ambergris

Minerals: Diamond

Plants: Almond in flower

Associated Gods: Ptah, Zeus, Ymir, Brahman

The Station of Kether

The Sephirotic guide of Kether in the Tree Walk may be either a man or woman. The guide is not seen by the Tree Walkers, but is instead seated immediately behind the enclosed station of Kether. Only one Tree Walker may enter the station of Kether at a time. The station of Kether is composed of a pyramidal frame that is completely covered by a piece of white cloth. The cloth should be arranged in such a way to permit the Tree Walkers to enter the structure on one side and close the cloth behind them. The structure should be big enough to allow a person to sit or kneel inside comfortably without feeling cramped. The entire structure should be concealed from the view of the Tree Walkers until each individual is brought to the structure by the guide. This can be done using a hinged screen or veil. The station of Kether could also be in an entirely different room from the rest of the Sephirotic stations.

Inside the structure should be a single white pillar candle or votive candle (placed or covered with a glass so as not to be a fire hazard). There should also be a small mirror, hanging at eye level with the seated Tree Walker who enters therein (see Figure 17).

The Sephirotic guide, upon hearing a Tree Walker enter the structure, has the choice of saying one of the following phrases to each person who enters the station of Kether.

1) *"Behold, the Face of God"*; or 2) *"Behold, the Face of God. I am the first and the last. What I am, you cannot understand. Know this: I am that I am. There is nothing else. And at the end of all time, I shall still be."*

At this point the Tree Walker may leave the structure and permit the next person to enter. Some individuals may choose to sit for a few moments of meditation or to converse further with the Sephirotic guide, who should be flexible enough to offer personalized words of advice or wisdom. The guide should not let one individual Tree Walker take up too much time within the station, with a gentle instruction such as *"You may go now."*

The station of Kether should be perceived by the Tree Walkers as the essence of the spiritual quest—soothing and centered, yet also enigmatic.

Symbolism

Guide: Male or Female

Robe Color: white

Secondary Color: Black (headband, headdress, belt, sash, collar, etc.)

Lamen Symbol: Either a point within a circle or the number one in black against a background of white

Props and Additional Symbols: A chair for the guide behind the Kether structure. The structure itself should ideally be made of a pyramidal frame, such as the kind sold in New Age stores for the purpose of meditation. If this is not available, a similar frame can be built out of wood and hinged so that it is collapsible. Other items can be used for this purpose, such as a large tripod, or even a folding ladder. A large white cloth or sheets are used to cover the structure. (Note: It may be possible to simply hang the cloth from the ceiling and form the required pyramidal space. If you have access to a military supply store, a white parachute can be purchased for this purpose.)

A small mirror. A white pillar candle. A small rug to be placed inside the structure.

Endnotes

1. We once performed the Tree Walk in a large three-bedroom house, placing two complimentary Sephirorth in each bed room, two in the parlor, one in the kitchen, and one in the dining room.

2. From "The Temple of Nature" by David Vedder.

3. Taken from"The Phases of the Moon,"published in *A Vision*, by W. B. Yeats.

4. The *Emerald Tablet* is also called the *Tabula Smaragdina*. The works of Hermes Trismegistus were the inspiration behind the Western Esoteric Tradition--the mystical/magical tradition of the western world, which focuses on Kabbalah and spiritual alchemy.

5. This discourse is taken from a short piece called "The Thunder, Perfect Mind," one of the ancient Gnostic writings unearthed at Nag Hammadi.

6. Taken from the Adeptus Minor Ritual of the Golden Dawn.

7. Based on "The Bornless Ritual" of the Golden Dawn, which was in turn based on an invocation known as "The Stele of Jeu the Hieroglyphist in his letter," from the Graeco-Egyptian Magical Papyri, a collection of magical texts that date from the second to fifth centuries C.E.

8. Shakespeare, *Merchant of Venice, IV, 1*.

9. Dekker, *Patient Grissil: Lullaby*.

10. An untitled poem by R. Buckminster Fuller, published in *No More Secondhand God*.

11. Mary Daly, *Beyond God the Father*.

12. George Bernard Shaw, published in *Collected Letters*.

13. Johann Kasper Lavater, *Aphorisms on Man*.

CHAPTER FOUR

THE PATHS

Connecting the Sephiroth are various pathways, channels or conduits, which are usually referred to as the paths. As stated earlier, the twenty-two paths that link the spheres follow the winding path of the Serpent of Wisdom. The Hebrew word for "paths" is *Nativoth*, a word that indicates a private or personal path, as opposed to a public thoroughfare. They are hidden paths that are to be accessed by the individual through meditation, visualization, and other forms of magical work.

The Sephiroth are the various objective levels of the manifestation of the divine light or the evolution of divine energy. The paths, on the other hand, are levels of subjective consciousness that can be utilized by the individual soul in its quest to understand cosmic manifestation and divine awareness. The rest areas along this quest are the Sephiroth—the different routes that

Path	Between	Letter	Meaning	Pronounced	English Letter	Value	Tarot Card	Attribute
11	Kether / Chokmah	א Aleph	ox	ah-lef	a	1	Fool	
12	Kether / Binah	ב Beth	house	beth	b	2	Magician	
13	Kether / Tiphareth	ג Gimel	camel	gih-mel	g, gh	3	High Priestess	
14	Chokmah / Binah	ד Daleth	door	dah-leth	d, dh	4	Empress	
15	Chokmah / Tiphareth	ה Heh	window	hay	h	5	Emperor	
16	Chokmah / Chesed	ו Vav	nail	vahv/vah	v, o, w	6	Hierophant	
17	Binah / Tiphareth	ז Zayin	sword	zah-yeen	z	7	Lovers	
18	Binah / Geburah	ח Cheth	fence	chayth	ch	8	Chariot	
19	Chesed / Geburah	ט Teth	serpent	tayth	t	9	Strength	
20	Chesed / Tiphareth	י Yod	hand	yohd	i, y	10	Hermit	
21	Chesed / Netzach	כ Kaph	palm/fist	kahf	k, kh	20*	Wheel of Fortune	
22	Geburah / Tiphareth	ל Lamed	ox goad	lah-med	l	30	Justice	
23	Geburah / Hod	מ Mem	water	mem	m	40*	Hanged Man	
24	Tiphareth / Netzach	נ Nun	fish	noon	n	50*	Death	
25	Tiphareth / Yesod	ס Samekh	prop	sah-mek	s	60	Temperance	
26	Tiphareth / Hod	ע Ayin	eye	ah-yeen	aa	70	Devil	
27	Netzach / Hod	פ Peh	mouth	pay	p, ph	80*	Tower	
28	Netzach / Yesod	צ Tzaddi	fish hook	tsah-dee	tz, ts	90*	Star	
29	Netzach / Malkuth	ק Qoph	back of head	kohf	q	100	Moon	
30	Hod / Yesod	ר Resh	head	raysh	r	200	Sun	
31	Hod / Malkuth	ש Shin	tooth	sheen	s, sh	300	Judgment	
32	Yesod / Malkuth	ת Tau	cross	tau	t, th	400	Universe	

*Final letters (when used at the end of a word): Kaph ך = 500, Mem ם = 600, Nun ן = 700, Peh ף = 800, Tzaddi ץ = 900

130

lead there are the paths, each with its own particular scenery. But each path is to be trodden alone, and each experience along the way will be unique to the individual traveler. In traversing these paths, however, it is necessary that we begin at the bottom of the Tree and work our way back to the point of our origin, following the meandering trail of the Serpent from Malkuth to Kether. Thus all students explore the paths beginning with the final one, the Thirty-second Path of Tau.

Like the Sephiroth, the paths that connect them have numerous correspondences and archetypal images. The paths may be visualized as hollow pipes that link brilliant transparent orbs of radiating color. These twenty-two paths are attributed to the twenty-two letters of the Hebrew alphabet. Each path is also associated with one of the following: an element, a planet, or a zodiacal sign. Additional correspondences include Tarot Trumps and numeral values. Through these different passageways and their many attributions, the student can ascend from one sphere to the next, encountering the divine light with ever greater clarity.

The list below gives numerous path correspondences, which should prove helpful to the reader. Following that is a brief description of the twenty-two paths.

The 32nd Path, Tau

Yetziratic Title in Hebrew: Sekhel Ne'evad

Yetziratic Title in English: The Administrative Intelligence

Hebrew Letter: Tau (meaning "cross")

Position on the Tree: Between Yesod and Malkuth

Usual Color: Blue-violet

Attribution: The element of earth. The planet Saturn.

Spiritual Experience: The vision of Destiny. The descent into the Underworld.

Magical Phenomenon: Geomancy, Alchemy

Tarot Trump: The Universe

Virtues: Introspection, Fulfillment

Vices: Self-limiting, Melancholy

Symbols: A "T"-Cross, a cave, the zodiac

Magical Weapons: a pantacle, a sickle

Scent: Storax

Minerals: Salt, onyx

Plants: Oak, ivy, ash, cypress, yew, nightshade

Animal: Crocodile, bull

Musical Note: A natural

Associated Gods: Mut, Osiris, Nephthys, Cronos, Saturn, Gaea, Demeter

The Thirty-second Path is the Administrative Intelligence, and it is so called because it directs and associates the motions of the seven planets, directing all of them in their own proper courses.

This "Administrative Intelligence" is a force that governs, "directs and associates" everything in the cosmos. The "seven planets" not only refer to celestial bodies of the greater universe, but also to the constituent parts of a lesser universe, the human psyche, which the Thirty-second Path directs "all of them in their own proper courses."

This path is the point at which students begin to explore the Tree of Life, as well as their own inner selves. The Thirty-second path is a portal from the physical world (Malkuth) to the astral plane (Yesod). As such, this path is also the first step to mystic and psychic awareness. Thus, we begin the journey in our physical forms, yet we turn our minds to the incorporeal worlds. On this path we must learn to accept the fact that the divine god-force is present in the physical environment just as much as it is in the celestial realms.

Traveling upon this route has been likened to a journey through the underworld, which is symbolic of the subconscious. A pilgrimage through the underworld of one's own unconscious mind is a trek through a land full of shadows and ghosts of one's own making. These "personal phantoms" must be sufficiently dealt with—assimilated or reconciled—before any spiritual progress is made.

The letter of this path, Tau, is the final letter of the Hebrew alphabet. The letters Aleph-Tau are symbolic of the beginning and the end, just as "A to Z" or "Alpha and Omega." Tau means "cross," an emblem used for marking, sealing, or signing. The path of Tau is therefore the *beginning* of a new (spiritual) type of existence, and the *completion* of an old (mundane) one. On the Tree of Life, the Thirty-second path marks or *seals* the end of divine manifestation. In the student who ascends through the path of Tau, it is a mark or seal of a new mystical life or viewpoint.

The 31st Path, Shin

Yetziratic Title in Hebrew: Sekhel Temidi

Yetziratic Title in English: The Perpetual Intelligence

Hebrew Letter: Shin (meaning "tooth")

Position on the Tree: Between Hod and Malkuth

Usually Colored: Red

Attribution: The element of fire. The element of spirit

Spiritual Experience: The vision of Transformation, Metamorphosis

Magical Phenomenon: Evocation, pyromancy

Tarot Trump: Judgment

Virtues: Passion, decisiveness, purity

Vices: Over-critical, resistance, fear of consequences

Symbols: A fiery altar, the trumpet, resurrection, the pyramid of flame

Magical Weapons: The wand, the lamp

Scent: Olibanum, frankincense, copal

Minerals: Fire opal

Plants: Red poppy, hibiscus

Animal: Lion, sphinx

Musical Note: C natural

Associated Gods: Ptah, Mau, Phoenix, Vulcan, Pluto, Hades

> *The Thirty-first Path is the Perpetual Intelligence; but why is it so called? Because it regulates the motions of the Sun and Moon in their proper order, each in an orbit convenient for it.*

The Thirty-first Path "regulates the motions of the Sun and the Moon," luminaries which are analogous to male and female polarities of energy. "Each in an orbit convenient for it" suggests that these energies are separated in an alchemical fashion in order that both may be systematically purified and recombined into a greater unity. That this path is known as the "Perpetual Intelligence" indicates that this is a continual process that requires constant attention and care.

This path links and harmonizes the corporeal energies of Malkuth with the intellectual powers of Hod. It is a connection between the body and the rational mind. This is the route taken by the lower personality as it struggles to become aware of its own internal mechanisms. While the student traveling this path advances ever nearer to the object of his desire, all imperfections are gradually incinerated by the purifying fire of Shin—the holy fire of the Divine. Only the balanced and pure portions remain. The result is a type of resurrection or rebirth, where the various parts of the lower personality are studied and appraised by the logical mind. This is a stage of psychic awareness where the normal waking consciousness begins to realize that it is not isolated from the spiritual energies that surround it. However, the student must constantly determine what is rational versus what is instinctive, and be able to balance experience with logic.

The 30th Path, Resh

Yetziratic Title in Hebrew: Sekhel Kelali

Yetziratic Title in English: The Collecting Intelligence

Hebrew Letter: Resh (meaning "head")

Position on the Tree: Between Hod and Yesod

Usually Colored: Orange

Attribution: Sol, the sun

Spiritual Experience: The vision of the Divine Intellect. Analysis

Magical Phenomenon: Healing

Tarot Trump: The Sun

Virtues: Clear thinking, Self-discovery, Rejuvenation

Vices: Insensitivity, destruction

Symbols: Children, the sun, a wall, a sunflower, a unicorn

Magical Weapons: The lamen

Scent: Olibanum, frankincense, copal

Minerals: Chrysolite, gold

Plants: Sunflower, laurel, heliotrope

Animal: Sparrow-hawk, lion

Musical Note: D natural

Associated Gods: Re, Aten, Shamash, Helios, Apollo, Christos, Mithras

> *The Thirtieth Path is the Collecting Intelligence, and is so called because Astrologers deduce from it the judgment of the stars and celestial signs, and the perfections of their science, according to the rules of the motions of the stars.*

The "Collecting Intelligence" implies accumulation, increase, and growth. The Hebrew letter Resh is attributed to the Sun and the "head," which suggests both cosmic and human consciousness. This is therefore a path of increasing levels of consciousness, where all forms of consciousness are collected, integrated, and appropriated for a divine purpose. Here are established the laws that rule our notions of reality. "The judgment of the stars and celestial signs, and the perfections of their science, according to the rules of the motions of the stars" indicates the precise structure and operation of cosmic law, which rules and regulates all things in the universe. Therefore the evolution (increase) of human consciousness acts "according to the rules" of cosmic or eternal consciousness.

The Thirtieth Path leads from the astral, imaginative world in Yesod, to the sphere of the rational mind in Hod. It is therefore a conducting path of the thought process or intellectual energy that further refines the lower personality of the student. The path of Resh is a balance between the imagination and the intellect. But here our consciousness turns inward for guidance and support. Here we endeavor to harvest true inner sight, purged from all psychological obstacles that stand in the way of growth. A sense of regeneration or rejuvenation is the gift that the divine consciousness bestows on this path.

Since Hebrew letter Resh means "head," it further alludes to the function of the "Collecting Intelligence," assembling information and experiences that the personality can use in its quest for something higher. This is the place where mind and body—logic and intuition—must be balanced. The physical must be reconciled with the mental, and this process is aided by the intervention of the divine mind, sought from within. The Thirtieth Path is also where intimate communication with the so-called Illuminated Masters or Inner Planes Contacts takes place.

The 29th Path, Qoph

Yetziratic Title in Hebrew: Sekhel Mughsham

Yetziratic Title in English: The Corporeal Intelligence

Hebrew Letter: Qoph (meaning "back of the head")

Position on the Tree: Between Netzach and Malkuth

Usually Colored: Red-violet

Attribution: Pisces

Spiritual Experience: The vision of Manifestation. Phenomenon

Magical Phenomenon: Bewitchments

Tarot Trump: The Moon

Virtues: Intuition, Imagination

Vices: Hallucination, Escapism

Symbols: The moon, two dogs, two towers, the crayfish, phantoms

Magical Weapons: The magic mirror

Scent: Ambergris, rose

Minerals: Pearl

Plants: Poppy

Animal: Dog, fish, amphibians

Musical Note: B natural

Associated Gods: Sin, Khonsu, Opowet, Dagon, Ea, Poseidon, Neptune, Hecate

The Twenty-ninth Path is the Corporeal Intelligence, so called because it forms every body which is formed in all the worlds, and the reproduction of them.

The "Corporeal Intelligence" denotes that the Twenty-ninth Path is concerned with "body consciousness" and "reproduction." The Hebrew letter Qoph means "back of the Head," and it is especially associated with those organs that control automatic motor functions and other involuntary or subconscious body functions. Qoph also suggests "sleep," another reference to the subconscious mind. There is a clear sexual connotation here as well, for the passage indicates that this path plays a major role in the procreation of "every body."

The Twenty-ninth Path runs between Netzach, the seat of the emotions, and Malkuth, the sphere of the "body" whose life functions are controlled by the motor impulses. Thus this path embodies the intuitive faculties, which are a by-product of the unconscious. It is the great unknown, the deep dark well of the subconscious—a source of some of our greatest visions, as well as our most repressed fears. The subconscious mind is a sanctuary where magicians and mystics can go to periodically withdraw from the outside world. To most people, this is secret place that is only entered while asleep in the dream-state, to be forgotten upon waking. But the magician can access this natural wellspring of inspiration and psychic fertility at any time though meditation and ritual work.

The path of Qoph is one of cycles, of ebb and flow. It is also one of evolution where the student experiences various levels of psychic development. One of the lessons of this path is that the mind and the body must work together for balance. The body is not to be looked upon as simply the gross container for the spirit. Body and spirit are not enemies. Both must work in harmony for true spiritual growth to occur.

The 28th Path, Tzaddi

Yetziratic Title in Hebrew: Sekhel Motba

Yetziratic Title in English: The Natural Intelligence

Hebrew Letter: Tzaddi (meaning "fish-hook")

Position on the Tree: Between Netzach and Yesod

Usually Colored: Violet

Attribution: Aquarius

Spiritual Experience: The vision of Harmony. Contemplation. Meditation

Magical Phenomenon: Astrology

Tarot Trump: The Star

Virtues: Patience, Inspiration

Vices: Indolence, Prone to fantasy

Symbols: The Water-bearer, the jar, the sistrum, the ibis, the star, the night sky, the river

Magical Weapons: The censer, the aspergillus

Scent: Galbanum, red sandalwood

Minerals: Glass, crystal

Plants: Olive, coconut

Animal: Eagle, peacock, man, ibis

Musical Note: A sharp

Associated Goddesses: Nuet, Isis, Ishtar, Aphrodite, Athena, Hera, Juno

> *The Twenty-eighth Path is called the Natural Intelligence; by it is completed and perfected the nature of all that exists beneath the Sun.*

The "Natural Intelligence" informs us that "all that exists beneath the Sun" is "natural." Even the things that we perceive as supernatural or abnormal, such as the powers of magic, divination, telekinesis, and other so-called supernormal events, are in fact totally natural. They belong to a nature that is "completed and perfected." Through our gradual evolution, what we regard today as mysterious occurrences may someday be explained as easily as the phenomena of lightning or the aurora borealis.

The Twenty-eighth Path connects the emotive mind in Netzach with the Astral Foundation in Yesod. It is therefore a path of deep meditation and contemplation. This is *focused meditation,* a higher form of the meditation found on the previous path. The process of focused meditation involves concentrating on certain symbols that act as portals to inner knowledge of the cosmos. Through meditation, one consciously participates in the expansion of universal understanding. The Hebrew letter Tzaddi means "fishhook," which alludes to the role this path plays in the act of meditation. The student uses the energies of this path to cast the fishhook (focused meditation) into the waters of the subconscious in order to catch a bit of divine knowledge. Included within that knowledge is the brief but profound realization that we are the subject of continuous contemplation by the divine life source on the nature of its own essence. In those short-lived moments where our meditations on the Divine come face to face with the Divine's meditations on us, true illumination occurs.

One of the tasks to be completed on this path is to learn that patience goes hand in hand with the practice of meditation. The student mustn't get discouraged if his meditations are not immediately fruitful. Like the fisherman who waits patiently for a nibble on the hook, the student must be diligent in his work.

The 27th Path, Peh

Yetziratic Title in Hebrew: Sekhel Morgash

Yetziratic Title in English: The Exciting Intelligence

Hebrew Letter: Peh (meaning "mouth")

Position on the Tree: Between Hod and Netzach

Usually Colored: Red

Attribution: The planet Mars

Spiritual Experience: The vision of Great Force. Vibration. Revision. The power of Speech

Magical Phenomenon: Retribution. Balance during transformation. Cosmic Force

Tarot Trump: The Tower

Virtues: Purification, Projection

Vices: Pessimism, Fear of Change

Symbols: The Tower of Babel, the bolt of lightning, the mouth

Magical Weapons: The sword

Scent: Pepper, Dragon's Blood resin, benzoin

Minerals: Ruby, garnet

Plants: Absinth, rue

Animal: Horse, bear, wolf

Musical Note: C natural

Associated Gods: Adad, Anhur, Horus, Mont, Sekhmet, Ares, Mars

> *The Twenty-seventh Path is the Active or Exciting Intelligence, and it is so called because through it every existent being receives its spirit and motion.*

The "Active or Exciting Intelligence" denotes a great flurry of cosmic activity on the path that runs between Netzach (emotions/fire) and Hod (intellect/water).

This lowermost of the horizontal paths reflects the whirling motions that produced Kether from the Limitless Light at a low level on the Tree where all energies are more clearly felt by "every existent being" in the physical realm. Through the activity of the Exciting Intelligence, all created beings are vitalized with "motion" and infused with "spirit."

The Hebrew letter Peh means "mouth," which is the vehicle for speech and the intonation of words and sounds. The power of the letter Peh is that of vibration. All particles of matter are said to have their own vibratory rate. This oscillation of energy is part of what defines one substance from another substance. The letter Peh is a symbol of the materialization of abstract thought forms through the vibrated word. Magicians tap into this power by learning how to vibrate god names and other words of power.

The "Active Intelligence" of this path seems destructive to us, but in reality, this is merely the process of disintegration—the breaking down of the old in favor of the new, just as the breaking down of fossil fuels releases a great amount of energy. It is a reapportioning of energy brought about by vibration. The universe itself is powered by this continual cycle of demolition and renewal.

The tasks of the student on the Twenty-seventh Path are twofold. First he must harness the power of the spoken word, and relinquish old outmoded forms or ideas and let new ones evolve. But in addition, the traveler on this path must strive to maintain a healthy balance between emotions (Netzach) and intellect (Hod).

The 26th Path, Ayin

Yetziratic Title in Hebrew: Sekhel Mechudash

Yetziratic Title in English: The Renovating Intelligence

Hebrew Letter: Ayin (meaning "eye")

Position on the Tree: Between Tiphareth and Hod

Usually Colored: Blue-violet

Attribution: Capricorn

Spiritual Experience: The vision of Inner Sight. The power of Laughter. Knowledge of the Secret Force

Magical Phenomenon: Wish fulfillment

Tarot Trump: The Devil

Virtues: Perception, Reproduction

Vices: Deception, Perversity

Symbols: The Devil, the sexual organs, the inverted pentagram, chains

Magical Weapons: The lamp, the Secret Force

Scent: Musk, civet

Minerals: Black diamond

Plants: Hemp, orchis root, thistle

Animal: Goat, ass

Musical Note: A natural

Associated Gods: Set, Mendes, Pan, Priapus, Bacchus

> *The Twenty-sixth Path is called the Renewing Intelligence, because the Holy God renews by it all the changing things which are renewed by the creation of the world.*

The "Renewing Intelligence" implies reproduction, re-creation, and rejuvenation. This is physical renewal as the divine life force isssues from Tiphareth into the form-building sphere of Hod, but also the renovation of consciousness which, even as it undergoes the process of renewal, still maintains a fundamental composition that the student must strive to rise above.

The Hebrew letter Ayin means "eye." This refers both to the physical eyes and the invisible "third" eye, and it points out the differences between outer mundane vision and true inner sight. Any sleight-of-hand magician can demonstrate how easily the physical eyes can be deceived. True inner vision, on the other hand, cannot be so easily fooled. On this path one must be careful not to confuse the outer corporeal form for the inward reality. Reproduction of physical form is attributed here, so it is on this path that the student can be deluded by the illusion of the material. Although the realm of matter is very important to the stability of the universe, appearances can be deceiving. Here the student must look beyond the form in Hod to perceive the Light of Tiphareth.

The 25th Path, Samekh

Yetziratic Title in Hebrew: Sekhel Nisyoni

Yetziratic Title in English: The Intelligence of Probation

Hebrew Letter: Samekh (meaning "prop" or "support")

Position on the Tree: Between Tiphareth and Yesod

Usually Colored: Blue

Attribution: Sagittarius

Spiritual Experience: The vision of Temptation. Trial. The Dark Night of the Soul

Magical Phenomenon: Transmutations

Tarot Trump: Temperance

Virtues: Endurance, verification

Vices: Lack of discrimination, Self-doubt

Symbols: The Angel, the rainbow, the vases, the cauldron, the bow and arrows

Magical Weapons: The arrow

Scent: lign-aloes

Minerals: Jacinth

Plants: Rush, iris

Animal: Centaur, horse, hippogriff

Musical Note: G sharp

Associated Gods: Neith, Artemis, Diana, Chiron, Apollo

The Twenty-fifth Path is the Intelligence of Proba-
tion, or Temptation, and it is so called because it is
the primary temptation, by which the Creator tri-
eth all righteous persons.

The "Intelligence of Probation or Temptation" indicates that this is a path where students must use discrimination and constantly test the veracity of their
spiritual beliefs through a process of trial and error,
careful measurement, frequent tests, and tribulations.
Just as a sword is "tempered" in fire and water, the
student on the Twenty-fifth Path between the fire of
the Sun (Tiphareth) and the water of the Moon
(Yesod) is tempered, strengthened, and balanced by
the constant rhythmical application of opposite influences. By administering "temptations" the Creator
strengthens the soul of the student so that it becomes
a fit and resilient vessel for the divine life force, and so
it has the ability to know what is true and remain in a
state of perfect balance.

The Hebrew letter Samekh means "prop" or "support," which implies divine guidance in the face of
temptation. Here the student's beliefs are confirmed
by effort and the overcoming of adversity. On the
Twenty-fifth Path the student who perseveres comes
into contact with the higher self and experiences the
presence of the divine. When a person truly experiences the energies of this mystical path, by-passing
the various temptations that obstruct growth, the
result is an exalted state of consciousness wherein
nothing looks exactly as it did before.

The 24th Path, Nun

Yetziratic Title in Hebrew: Sekhel Dimyoni

Yetziratic Title in English: The Imaginative Intelligence

Hebrew Letter: Nun (meaning "fish")

Position on the Tree: Between Tiphareth and Netzach

Usually Colored: Blue-green

Attribution: Scorpio

Spiritual Experience: The vision of Rebirth. Transformation. Reproduction

Magical Phenomenon: Spirit communications

Tarot Trump: Death

Virtues: Transcendence, Liberation

Vices: Resistance, Fear

Symbols: The skeleton, the scythe, the serpent, the scorpion, the eagle

Scent: Benzoin, opoponax

Minerals: Snakestone

Plants: Cactus

Animal: Scorpion, eagle, fish, beetle, wolf, jackal

Musical Note: G natural

Associated Gods: Khephra, Apep, Osiris, Pluto, Cybele

The Twenty-fourth Path is the Imaginative Intelligence, and it is so called because it gives a likeness to all the similitudes which are created in like manner similar to its harmonious elegancies.

The Hebrew word *dimyoni*, "imaginative," is closely related to the word *dimyon*, which means "semblance, likeness." This passage indicates that by uniting opposites, a greater wholeness is achieved. A fresh synthesis arises that creates new versions of itself, all of which have a similarity or semblance to the "harmonious elegancies" of the divine life force. "For the outward form always follows the Hidden Law, thus from Chaos is produced Harmony, just as a beautiful flower is produced from decaying matter."[1] The Imaginative Intelligence constantly creates new images that we may use to aid us in our spiritual quest, just as humanity itself was created in the "image" of the Divine.

The Hebrew letter Nun means "fish," which is the object desired by the "fishhook" (Tzaddi/meditation). This letter is also associated with the ideas of water (consciousness) and the Sun (the Christos as a solar deity symbolized by a fish). Nun also has correspondences with the ideas of generation and fecundity.

The Twenty-fourth Path leads from Netzach, the seat of the imaginative consciousness, to Tiphareth, the seat of the Sun. It is therefore the path of hidden energies that, when aroused, lead to increasing levels of illumination. Here the student begins to forgo the desires of Netzach for the more universal love of

Tiphareth. The wants of the lower personality are forfeited for higher spiritual needs as the student's perceptions of reality and the purpose of life are constantly changing on this path. Outmoded ideas of the "self" evaporate as new self-images form to replace them.

The task of the student on this path is to let go of the old and yield to that which is unfamiliar, trusting in the love of the divine.

The 23rd Path, Mem

Yetziratic Title in Hebrew: Sekhel Qayyam

Yetziratic Title in English: The Stable Intelligence

Hebrew Letter: Mem (meaning "water")

Position on the Tree: Between Geburah and Hod

Usually Colored: Blue

Attribution: The element of water

Spiritual Experience: The vision of Sacrifice. Trance. Renewal. Release

Magical Phenomenon: The Great Work, talismans, scrying

Tarot Trump: The Hanged Man

Virtues: Serenity, Self-sacrificing

Vices: Self-abusive, Withdrawn

Symbols: The hanged man, the tree or frame, water

Magical Weapons: The Cup and Cross of Suffering, the Wine

Scent: Onycha, myrrh

Minerals: Aquamarine

Plants: Lotus, all water plants

Animal: eagle

Musical Note: G sharp

Associated Gods: Oannes, Dagon, Ea, Poseidon, Neptune, Osiris, Christos

> *The Twenty-third Path is the Stable Intelligence, and it is so called because it has the virtue of consistency among all numerations.*

The "Stable Intelligence" denotes an attitude of stillness and fixed purpose. This path runs between the fiery sphere of Geburah and the watery realm of Hod. Geburah restricts, while Hod expands. One could expect this to be a turbulent path, and indeed the idea of self-sacrifice that is associated here points out what pressures are involved. The opposing energies of the two spheres are forced into compliance with one another, resulting in stability and "the virtue of *consistency* among all numerations" (the Sephiroth).

The Hebrew letter Mem means "water," a symbol of the universal consciousness which is maternal and nourishing. The Twenty-third Path represents a "baptism" in the intuitive, feminine element of water—a kind of return to the stability of the eternal womb.

Water is also the element that purifies and dissolves. Thus this path is one of intense transformation and purification—away from the influences of the outer secular world.

On this path the watery intellect of Hod is the vehicle for profound mental focus, while the fire of Geburah lends unwavering justice. The result is single-minded purpose and devotion, which permits the student to become a purified vessel for divine truth.

The student who journeys upon the Twenty-third Path learns to sacrifice lower wants and desires for something nobler, higher, and more permanent.

The 22nd Path, Lamed

Yetziratic Title in Hebrew: Sekhel Ne'eman

Yetziratic Title in English: The Faithful Intelligence

Hebrew Letter: Lamed (meaning "ox-goad")

Position on the Tree: Between Tiphareth and Geburah

Usually Colored: Green

Attribution: Libra

Spiritual Experience: The vision of Equilibration. Uprightness. Self-assessment

Magical Phenomenon: All works of Justice and Balance

Tarot Trump: Justice

Virtues: Integrity, Responsibility

Vices: Perfunctory, quick to pass judgment

Symbols: The winged goddess, the scales, the sword, the feather, wings

Magical Weapons: The Cross of Equilibrium

Scent: Galbanum

Minerals: Emerald

Plants: Aloe

Animal: Elephant

Musical Note: F sharp

Associated Gods: Maat, Themis, Minos

> *The Twenty-second Path is the Faithful Intelligence, and it is so called because by it spiritual virtues are increased, and all dwellers on earth are nearly under its shadow.*

The "Faithful Intelligence" relates this path to the concept of amen or "faith." Amen also has the additional meanings of "so mote it be," "loyalty," and "steadfastness." Those who remain faithful or loyal to the will of the Eternal benefit from this allegiance by receiving an increase in "spiritual virtues." They also receive divine protection by dwelling under the "shadow" of the Eternal. The Faithful Intelligence increases and dispenses the energies of the divine life force in an equilibrating and just manner.

The Hebrew letter Lamed means "ox goad," a tool used to guide an ox in the proper direction and out of harm's way. By analogy, the divine life force uses the energies of the Twenty-second Path to guide us and teach us what we are to learn on our quest. Sometimes the lessons students must learn are harsh but necessary. The Sword of Justice always keeps us on the right path, ever moving forward in our spiritual progression.

This path, leading from the sphere of perfect equilibrium (Tiphareth) to that of severity (Geburah) maintains the balance of the entire Tree of Life. And the challenge for students traveling this route is to educate themselves through inner knowledge gained through meditative practice. They must put that knowledge to use and maintain their own sense of balance through the perpetual correction and regulation of thoughts and deeds. Prodded on toward the correct path by karma, the student must make an effort to retrain his thoughts and calibrate his actions to better reflect the grace and equilibrium of the Divine.

The 21st Path, Kaph

Yetziratic Title in Hebrew: Sekhel ha-Chaphutz ha-Mevuqash

Yetziratic Title in English: The Intelligence of Conciliation and Reward

Hebrew Letter: Kaph (meaning "palm of the hand" or "closed hand")

Position on the Tree: Between Chesed and Netzach

Usually Colored: Violet

Attribution: The planet Jupiter

Spiritual Experience: The vision of Circumstance. Karma

Magical Phenomenon: Social ascendancy, balanced spirituality

Tarot Trump: The Wheel of Fortune

Virtues: Perseverance, charity

Vices: Entrapment, apathy

Symbols: The wheel, the grail, the round table, the sphinx

Magical Weapons: The scepter

Scent: Saffron

Minerals: Amethyst, lapis lazuli

Plants: Hyssop, oak, poplar, fig

Animal: Eagle, ox, lion, man, baboon, dog-headed ape

Musical Note: A sharp

Associated Gods: Zeus, Cronus, Jupiter, Amoun

> *The Twenty-first Path is the Intelligence of Concili-*
> *iation and Reward, and is so called because it*
> *receives the divine influence which flows into it*
> *from its benediction upon all and each existence.*

This is a path that requires great exertion and true dedication to the spiritual quest. It is the road of aspiration that can only be tackled by true students. The Hebrew word *Mevuqash* implies something that is requested and sought after. The "conciliation" implies a new understanding or union between the higher and lower parts of the personality—they are no longer fighting each other or reaching for separate goals. Instead, they work in unison to "receive the divine influence that flows into it from its *benediction*" (Chesed). Reconciliation with the higher is the ultimate "reward"—the only thing that can satisfy the soul's hunger.

The Hebrew letter Kaph means "palm of the hand," something that is outstretched in the act of seeking or grasping, for the Twenty-first Path is not a route for the passive individual who wishes to sit back and let the world come to him. The emotion of Netzach gazes up at the loving mercy in Chesed, and a strong undeniable desire for the Divine is the result.

This is the path of the quest itself—the search for meaning and the essence of God. Though it may take many lifetimes to reach the goal, the student must endure, even though circumstances may place obstacles in one's path. The trick is to not allow personal circumstance to rule over one's destiny.

The challenge for the student on this quest is to tenaciously wait out all obstacles, until the natural rhythmic cycle of the universe causes a change in circumstances that will allow progress once more.

The 20th Path, Yod

Yetziratic Title in Hebrew: Sekhel ha-Ratzon

Yetziratic Title in English: The Intelligence of Will

Hebrew Letter: Yod (meaning "hand")

Position on the Tree: Between Tiphareth and Chesed

Usually Colored: Yellow-green

Attribution: Virgo

Spiritual Experience: The vision of Succor. Sustenance. Divine guidance

Magical Phenomenon: Invisibility, parthenogenesis, initiation

Tarot Trump: The Hermit

Virtues: Responsiveness, realignment

Vices: Isolation, irresolution

Symbols: The Hermit, the robe, the wand, the lamp, the serpent, the egg, the virgin

Magical Weapons: The lamp, the staff, the bread of life

Scent: Narcissus

Minerals: Peridot

Plants: Snowdrop, lily

Animal: lamb, all solitary animals

Musical Note: F natural

Associated Gods: Isis, Harparkrat, Attis, Ceres, Adonis

The Twentieth Path is the Intelligence of Will, and is so called because it is the means of preparation of all and each created being, and by this intelligence the existence of the Primordial Wisdom becomes known.

The "Intelligence of Will" denotes that this is the path where each individual "created being" is "prepared" for the spiritual quest by being made aware of the higher and divine "will" of the creator. By spiritual preparation (prayer, meditation, visualization, and aspiration) the student becomes aware of the higher will and ultimately attains oneness with the divine self—fully immersed in the knowledge of "the existence of the Primordial Wisdom."

The Hebrew letter Yod means "hand," and it refers to the hand of the Divine, extended to assist us. Yod is the primary letter whose shape forms the basis for all other Hebrew letters. This shape resembles a point, the beginning point of all created form. It also resembles a sperm, the primary cell of procreation. The value of Yod is ten, the number of perfection, for everything beyond ten returns again to units.

The Twentieth Path leads from the higher self in Tiphareth to the merciful love in Chesed. The seat of balance and beauty has been attained, but a higher divine love still beckons with an open hand. The path of Yod alludes to the self-created source of the universe. It is the path of adepthood, of union with the primordial source, the greater self of the universe. The path of

Yod is the route of introspection and individuation—it must be traveled alone. Here the magician learns to separate himself from the "herd mentality" that rules the lives of most people. This is a path that requires the determination to take up the quest on one's own. No one can make this journey for us. We must do it ourselves. Yet once the student has attained the level of self-realization symbolized by this route, the challenge is then to extend a helping hand to the next student who journeys up the path.

The 19th Path, Teth

Yetziratic Title in Hebrew: Sekhel Sod ha-Pauloth ha-Ruachnioth

Yetziratic Title in English: The Intelligence of the Secret of all Spiritual Activities

Hebrew Letter: Teth (meaning "serpent")

Position on the Tree: Between Chesed and Geburah

Usually Colored: Yellow

Attribution: Leo

Spiritual Experience: The vision of Secret Power

Magical Phenomenon: Taming wild creatures

Tarot Trump: Strength

Virtues: Willpower, Self-reliance

Vices: Wavering, Subservient, fearful

Symbols: The Lion, the maiden, the column, the
   sword, the serpent

Magical Weapon: Discipline

Scent: Olibanum

Minerals: Cat's eye

Plants: Sunflower

Animal: Lion, serpent

Musical Note: E natural

Associated Gods: Bast, Sekhmet, Mau, Venus, Demeter, Hercules

> *The Nineteenth Path is the Intelligence of the Secret*
> *of all the activities of the spiritual beings, and is so*
> *called because of the influence diffused by it from the*
> *most high and exalted sublime glory.*

The "secret activities" of the spiritual beings (or
angels) include the powers of number, expansion,
contraction, and vibration, those same forces that created the universe of the Sephiroth. By understanding
the nature of these secret activities and by working
with them, we are brought closer to these "beings."
This reciprocal (horizontal) path is a "diffused" counterpart of the influence of Kether, "the most high and
exalted sublime glory."

   The Hebrew letter Teth means "serpent," which in
Hebrew mysticism is a symbol of wisdom. It also represents a type of electromagnetic energy not unlike
that of the Eastern Kundalini. This "serpent power" is

used by mystics to activate the body's energy centers to cause a kind of divine rapture. The Nineteenth Path connects the Sephiroth of Chesed and Geburah, the primary spheres of water and fire on the Tree. Between these two polarities a natural electrical circuit is formed, which generates this vitalizing "serpent power" that is part of the magnetic current that powers the entire universe. The ability to direct and regulate this power is the basis for all occult work.

The goal of the traveler on this path is to learn how to exercise control over the various primal energies of both body and mind (instinctive tendencies, behavior patterns, etc.). The student must also be willing to face his deepest fears.

The 18th Path, Cheth

Yetziratic Title in Hebrew: Sekhel Beth ha-Shepha

Yetziratic Title in English: The Intelligence of the House of Influence

Hebrew Letter: Cheth (meaning "fence, enclosure")

Position on the Tree: Between Geburah and Binah

Usually Colored: Yellow-orange

Attribution: Cancer

Spiritual Experience: The vision of Triumph

Magical Phenomenon: Enchantments, visions

Tarot Trump: The Chariot

Virtues: Self-assurance, construction, receptivity

Vices: Pomposity, ego-inflation, deterioration

Symbols: The chariot, the sphinx, the fence, the castle, the moat

Magical Weapons: The Athanor

Scent: Onycha, myrhh

Minerals: Amber

Plants: Lotus, watercress

Animal: Crab, turtle, shellfish, sphinx, horse

Musical Note: C sharp

Associated Gods: Adad, Apollo, Helios, Odin, Harmachis, Khepera

> *The Eighteenth Path is called the Intelligence or House of Influence (by the greatness of whose abundance the influence of good things upon created beings is increased), and from its midst the arcana and hidden senses are drawn forth, which dwell in its shade and which cling to it, from the Causes of all causes.*

The "House of Influence" is the same as the "House of the Holy Spirit" which conducts to Binah the maternal sphere of "abundance" through which "the influx of good things upon created things is increased." From its station above the abyss, Binah is "hidden" to us, but its unseen influences are "drawn forth" through the Eighteenth Path to Geburah. The "shade" or shadow refers to the wings of the Holy One who protects and shelters us. (Under the shadow of Thy wings, Tetragrammaton.) As one of the three Supernals, the hidden influences "which cling to it" are closely connected to Kether, the "Cause of all causes."

The Hebrew letter Cheth means "fence," or "enclosure," which indicates the hidden nature of this path, as well as the idea of "containment." The containment referred to here are the diverse methods for organizing consciousness into forms that we can comprehend on a deep level. It represents a type of unconscious understanding that cannot be communicated by words—it is therefore "hidden" to all attempts by the conscious mind to define it in human language.

The idea of the "fence" in Cheth includes the image of the field that it encloses; they are not separate here. Division is useful to tell one thing apart from another thing—this is the basis of all conscious constructs of education and civilization. Division is a process of creation and growth (just as a cell divides and becomes two). However, Cheth teaches us not to become trapped in these divisions, because they are merely tools that help facilitate our understanding. Ultimate reality has no such divisions.

Seekers on the Eighteenth Path must realize that the outer form of the human being is in reality a container (Cheth) for the spirit or divine essence. Since *we* are the vessels that the divine spirit chooses to inhabit, it is important that we dedicate all aspects of ourselves toward eventual reunification with our eternal source. We must be receptive to the energies of the Divine. When this reunion is finally achieved, we will come to realize that there was no true separation in the first place.

The 17th Path, Zayin

Yetziratic Title in Hebrew: Sekhel ha-Hergesh

Yetziratic Title in English: The Disposing Intelligence

Hebrew Letter: Zayin (meaning "sword, armor")

Position on the Tree: Between Binah and Tiphareth

Usually Colored: Orange

Attribution: Gemini

Spiritual Experience: The vision of Prepared Work. Reconciliation. Union

Magical Phenomenon: Bi-location, Astral traveling, prophecy

Tarot Trump: The Lovers

Virtues: Preparation, organization

Vices: Separation, overburdened

Symbols: The twins, the sword, the helmet, the shield, the dragon

Magical Weapon: The tripod

Scent: Wormwood, violet

Minerals: Alexandrite, tourmaline

Plants: Orchids, hybrids

Animal: Dragon, Magpie, hybrids

Musical Note: D natural

Associated Gods: The twin Merti, Horus and Set, Isis
and Nephthys, Hermes, Mercury, Castor and
Pollux, Adam and Eve

> *The Seventeenth Path is the Disposing Intelli-*
> *gence, which provides Faith to the Righteous, and*
> *they are clothed with the Holy Spirit by it, and it is*
> *called the Foundation of Excellence in the state of*
> *higher things.*

This path "disposes" (arranges, prepares, or readies)
the Righteous by providing them with Faith. The
"Disposing Intelligence" implies that this path gives
constant adjustment, preparation, measurement,
judgment, and organization to the individual human
soul in order to make it ready for the final leap over
the abyss. At the summit of this path is Binah, the
sphere of the Holy Spirit. Those who are fit to truly
undertake this path are said to be "clothed with the
Holy Spirit." Through the Seventeenth Path,
Tiphareth, the seat of the Ruach (rational soul) and
the higher self, is joined to Binah, the seat of the
Neshamah (divine soul) and the subconscious mind.
The joining of the influences of these two Sephiroth
along this path results in its title of "the Foundation of
Excellence in the state of higher things."

The Hebrew letter Zayin means "sword," a
weapon that cuts and severs (or divides), thus it is
that type of god-energy that governs the process of
separation. As stated earlier, division is a method of

creation. Therefore, this is the path where the descending divine life force begins creation through division.

For the student who is ascending this path, it is a direct reversal of the process—where the separateness of the individual is dissolved into the unified whole of the divine. Duality is sacrificed. The various segments of the psyche (animus and anima, Ruach and Neshamah) become as one. The path of Zayin implies a period of self-analysis, followed by disposal of those elements of the psyche that are impure, until at length the component parts of the revitalized psyche are recombined into a greater unity. The result is intimacy and oneness with the divine.

The 16th Path, Vav

Yetziratic Title in Hebrew: Sekhel Nitzchi

Yetziratic Title in English: The Triumphal or Eternal Intelligence

Hebrew Letter: Vav (meaning "nail, hook")

Position on the Tree: Between Chokmah and Chesed

Usually Colored: Red-orange

Attribution: Taurus

Spiritual Experience: The vision of Great Revelation. Inner hearing

Magical Phenomenon: Physical strength

Tarot Trump: The Hierophant

Virtues: Endurance, Efficiency

Vices: Indolence, Materialism

Symbols: The bull, the Hierophant, the pope, the scepter, the cubic stone, a nail, a yoke, a phallus

Magical Weapons: The Labor of Preparation

Scent: Storax, musk

Minerals: Topaz

Plants: Mallow

Animal: Bull

Musical Note: C sharp

Associated Gods: Apis, Serapis, Osiris, Amoun, Hera, Venus, Mithras

> *The Sixteenth Path is the Triumphal or Eternal Intelligence, so called because it is the pleasure of the Glory, beyond which is no other Glory like to it, and it is called also the Paradise prepared for the Righteous.*

"Eternal" refers to the unfathomable Kether, whose energy begins to become tangible to us in the parental spheres of Chokmah and Binah, the father and mother principles. "Glory" is one of the titles of Chesed, and this path runs between Chokmah (Wisdom) and Chesed (Mercy/Greatness/Glory). "The pleasure of the Glory" refers to the harmonious influence of the divine energy as it is passed between these two similar spheres on the Pillar of Mercy. That it is the "Paradise prepared for the Righteous" indicates that this is a path of high spiritual ascension—the Paradise that is promised can only be obtained through discipline and virtue.

The Hebrew letter Vav means "nail" or "pin," a tool that fastens or joins. It also represents the conjunction "and," which points to its connecting attributes. The Sixteenth Path is a major conduit that crosses the abyss to connect the Supernals to the rest of the tree. It is a path through which divine wisdom (Chokmah) is transmitted to the lower spheres (the student). Thus it is our connecting link to Supernal unity. The faculty of hearing is attributed to this path. This is inner hearing—listening to the voice of the divine teacher within. Here, knowledge is given as a revelation. And the path of Vav is one of initiation.

On this path we must learn to still the inner "chatter" of our minds and strain to distinguish that one true inner voice of wisdom. This means that we are to sharpen our faculty of listening whenever we engage in meditation and ritual work.

The 15th Path, Heh

Yetziratic Title in Hebrew: Sekhel Maamid

Yetziratic Title in English: The Constituting Intelligence

Hebrew Letter: Heh (meaning "window")

Position on the Tree: Between Chokmah and Tiphareth

Usually Colored: Red

Attribution: Aries

Spiritual Experience: The vision of Creation. The power of Organization

Magical Phenomenon: Consecration

Tarot Trump: The Emperor

Virtues: Authority. Service. Duty

Vices: Abuse of Power. Self-indulgence

Symbols: The king, the ram, the sacrificial lamb, the orb of dominion

Magical Weapons: The burin, ram's horns

Scent: Dragon's blood, musk

Minerals: Ruby, star ruby

Plants: Tiger lily, geranium

Animal: Ram, hawk, owl

Musical Note: C natural

Associated Gods: Nergal, Mont, Khnemu, Ares, Mars, Athena, Minerva

> *The Fifteenth Path is the Constituting Intelligence, so called because it constitutes the substance of creation in pure darkness, and men have spoken of these contemplations; it is that darkness spoken of in Scripture, Job 38:9, "and thick darkness a swaddling band for it."*

"The substance of creation in pure darkness" refers to the creation of the world when the darkness of clouds hovered over the waters of the endless ocean. The world of light was created out of the darkness of nothingness. The "Constituting" Intelligence is that which establishes, sets up, arranges, and orders the world of light—the divine life force—that is born out of the dark womb with darkness itself as its swaddling clothes. Thus the Fifteenth Path constitutes the very structure, shape, and support of the Tree of Life.

The Hebrew letter Heh means "window," an opening that permits light and air into a building. The light is the light of divine wisdom, the air is the breath of the divine life force, and the building is the house (Beth) of the lower self. This letter is often said to be the letter that represents life and the nature of being. Heh also has an added correspondence with the faculty of sight. This "sight" implies watchfulness, investigation, and alertness. Heh is the window through which we can see the Divine.

The path of Heh establishes and arranges the divine life force—it brings cosmic order and divine law where once there was none. Heh also defines and classifies. Students traveling this path may experience feelings of introducing order and stability into disorderly situations. They may also start to categorize and arrange their conscious thoughts in a significant fashion. Students traveling on the Fifteenth Path should learn to depend on the Divine for its organization and form. They should also realize that we humans are not victims of fate, but rather, we are in control of our own personal destinies.

The 14th Path, Daleth

Yetziratic Title in Hebrew: Sekhel Meir

Yetziratic Title in English: The Illuminating Intelligence

Hebrew Letter: Daleth (meaning "door")

Position on the Tree: Between Chokmah and Binah

Usually Colored: Green

Attribution: The planet Venus

Spiritual Experience: The vision of Holiness. Divine Union

Magical Phenomenon: Love, realization through devotion

Tarot Trump: The Empress

Virtues: Devotion. Maternity

Vices: Conceit. Barrenness

Symbols: The mother, the winged goddess, the Holy Spirit, the dove, the ankh, wheat, pearls, the crown of stars, fleur-de-lis

Magical Weapons: The girdle

Scent: Sandalwood, violet

Minerals: Emerald, turquoise

Plants: Myrtle, rose, clover, acacia

Animal: Sparrow, dove, swan

Musical Note: F sharp

Associated Gods: Hathor, Isis, Inanna, Aphrodite, Venus, Demeter, Janus

The Fourteenth Path is the Illuminating Intelligence and is so called because it is that Chashmal (scintillating flame or brilliance) which is the founder of the concealed and fundamental ideas of holiness and of their stages of preparation.

The Fourteenth Path is a particular brilliance that is the founder (or foundation) of certain hidden, arcane spiritual energies. The term "foundation" draws an analogy to the sphere of Yesod, which is the foundation of life—the exact mechanics of which remain a mystery to us. They are "concealed." Life in this path is symbolized by the Chashmal, the scintillating flame. This divine life force is prepared in "stages" by the Fourteenth Path, which unites the Father (Chokmah) and the Mother (Binah), and results in the processes of conception and birth—the birth of the primal life force.

The Hebrew letter Daleth means "door." It is the portal or womb through which the life force is born. The path of Daleth organizes the energy from Chokmah and passes it along to Binah, the form-builder. It is our birth canal into this universe, the luminous and fruitful divine mother. Thus, it is a path of fertility—producing diverse mental images from the Divine. These images are the thought germs that give life to all manifestation in the cosmos. The path of Daleth is also a route of imagination, adaptation, and consciousness, as opposed to subconsciousness.

As one of the three reciprocal paths that straddles both sides of the Tree, this is a path that unites opposites. In this case it is the opposites of our archetypal creative forces symbolized by the logical male energy (Chokmah) and the intuitive female energy (Binah) that are united. When conscious reasoning and subconscious intuition are linked together, rather than at odds with each other, the result is fruitfulness and expansion. This can lead to new levels of awareness and increased powers of image visualization and imagination, which aid the student's spiritual growth. But in order to gain these benefits, we must learn to balance analytical thinking with intuitive insight, and try creative new approaches to our daily spiritual practice.

The 13th Path, Gimel

Yetziratic Title in Hebrew: Sekhel Manhig ha-Achdoth

Yetziratic Title in English: The Uniting or Conductive Intelligence

Hebrew Letter: Gimel (meaning "camel")

Position on the Tree: Between Kether and Tiphareth

Usually Colored: Blue

Attribution: Luna, the moon

Spiritual Experience: The vision of Wholeness. Truth

Magical Phenomenon: Clairvoyance, Divination by Dreams

Tarot Trump: The High Priestess

Virtues: Purity. Steadfastness

Vices: Inertia. Capriciousness

Symbols: The High Priestess, the Virgin Mother, the silver star, the crescent, the cup, the moon, the desert, the veil

Magical Weapons: The bow and arrow

Scent: Camphor, aloes, jasmine

Minerals: Moonstone, crystal, pearl

Plants: Almond, mugwort, hazel, moonwort

Animal: Dog, camel

Musical Note: G sharp

Associated Gods: Aah-Djehoti, Isis, Nuet, Sin, Ishtar, Artemis, Diana, Hecate, Selene

> *The Thirteenth Path is named the Uniting Intelligence, and is so called because it is itself the Essence of Glory. It is the Consummation of the Truth of individual spiritual things.*

This path is a direct pipeline that unites the human being (Tiphareth) to the divine self (Kether). It is the route of the soul. The Thirteenth Path, more than any other, is the path that connects the lesser universe of human to the greater universe of the Godhead. And because it is a clear, straight path between the major spheres of the head and the heart, it is the "Essence of Glory" that bestows a particular level of clarity and truth.

The Hebrew letter Gimel means "camel," an animal known for its stamina and ability to store water for long trips across the desert. The path of Gimel is the longest path on the Tree, and thus the symbol of the camel is appropriate. This path is sometimes said to be the only practical path that the student can use to reach Kether, since the paths of Beth and Aleph are primarily paths of energy descent. The Thirteenth Path, like the Twenty-fifth Path, can be a path of trial. The student who travels unswervingly along this longest of paths toward the ultimate goal of Kether can sometimes experience sensations of futility, isolation, and loneliness in the long stretches when the goal seems to be nowhere in sight.

The path of Gimel represents the purest root-essence of consciousness, often symbolized by water. The "Uniting Intelligence" knows and sees all. It is pure mental energy operating at the unconscious level. Its essence saturates all things in the universe, yet it remains unchanged by anything it touches. The Thirteenth Path is the primary regulator of the divine life force as it flows down the Tree in vibratory "waves" of energy that become ever more dense.

In traveling this path, the student attempts to unite the human part of the self to the divine part. Here the student also learns about the processes of memory (subconscious recall) and reflection (man as the counterpart of the Divine). Although this path may be a long ordeal, when it is finally accomplished the ultimate initiation takes place.

The 12th Path, Beth

Yetziratic Title in Hebrew: Sekhel Bahir

Yetziratic Title in English: The Intelligence of Transparency (or Light)

Hebrew Letter: Beth (meaning "house")

Position on the Tree: Between Kether and Binah

Usually Colored: Yellow

Attribution: The planet Mercury

Spiritual Experience: The vision of Perfection. Penetrating vision. The ability to discern

Magical Phenomenon: Knowledge of the sciences, miracles of healing, the gift of speech, high spiritual knowledge, seership

Tarot Trump: The Magician

Virtues: Concentration, intelligence

Vices: Untruthfulness, thoughtlessness

Symbols: The magician, the juggler, the altar, the infinity sign, the oroborous, the four elements

Magical Weapons: The caduceus, the wand

Scent: Mastic, white sandal, storax, mace

Minerals: Opal, agate

Plants: Vervain, palm

Animal: Swallow, ibis, ape

Musical Note: E natural

Associated Gods: Enki, Thoth, Hermes, Mercury, Odin

> *The Twelfth Path is the Intelligence of Transparency, because it is that species of Magnificence called Chazchazit (or seership), the place whence issues the vision of those seeing in apparitions.*

This path has a great deal to say about the idea of psychic vision. The "transparency" of the path implies a certain clarity that is needed for true revelation. It is the place of true prophecy or seership. This is not simply the lower psychic reflexes, but rather the pure and clear root of all higher spiritual visions. It is the revelation of the divine self as it emerges. From this vantage point one is able to observe the arcane workings of all dimensions through various methods of psychic awareness and inner sight.

The Hebrew letter Beth means "house." This indicates that the Twelfth Path is one of containment, sanctuary, or a place of "being within." It is the dwelling place of the Divine. Since it connects the pure consciousness in Kether to the maternal subconsciousness in Binah, this path represents the supreme self-consciousness that is the supreme "seer," who knows and sees all.

The Twelfth Path alludes to potential manifesting into action. Since Binah is the sphere that limits form by dividing and organizing it, the path of Beth partakes of this function as well, organizing the creative (potential) energy from Kether into manifestation in Binah. It represents the primal will of the Divine that is reflected in the purified will of mortal man seeking to unite with it. This divine will seeks to manifest itself into diverse ideas of form as it descends the Tree.

The student exploring this path should remember that the "seership" alluded to on this path is spiritual knowledge in its highest form. Although there is nothing wrong with exploring visionary gifts (clairvoyance, etc.), it is important not to become an "astral junky"— one who wanders aimlessly and carelessly on the astral planes. The key is to develop focused concentration, which allows the divine energy to be clearly seen.

The 11th Path, Aleph

Yetziratic Title in Hebrew: Sekhel Metzochtzoch

Yetziratic Title in English: The Scintillating or Fiery Intelligence

Hebrew Letter: Aleph (meaning "ox")

Position on the Tree: Between Kether and Chokmah

Usually Colored: Yellow

Attribution: The element of Air

Spiritual Experience: The vision of the Inexpressible, The vision of the Face of God

Magical Phenomenon: Divination

Tarot Trump: The Fool

Virtues: Self-assurance, awareness

Vices: Foolishness, obliviousness

Symbols: The fool, the jester, the rose, the cliff, the dog, the wolf

Magical Weapons: The dagger, the fan

Scent: Galbanum, ambergris

Minerals: Topaz, chalcedony

Plants: Peppermint, aspen

Animal: Eagle, man

Musical Note: E natural

Associated Gods: Nu, Hermes, Mercury, Harparkrat

> *The Eleventh Path is the Scintillating Intelligence, because it is the essence of that curtain which is placed close to the order of the disposition, and this is a special dignity given to it that it may be able to stand before the Face of the Cause of Causes.*

The above statement indicates that this path best reflects the first outflow of pure divine energy from Kether, the "cause of causes." Thus the path scintillates or shimmers with light. The first path beyond Kether is described as a curtain, a veil before the Holy of Holies which, by design, conceals the highest Sephirah from those who have not fully ascended to it. The Eleventh Path connects Kether with Chokmah, therefore it partakes of the same ineffable energy of Kether and the Ain Soph beyond. All energies that are above Chokmah are completely beyond human understanding.

The Hebrew letter Aleph means "ox." This refers to the primal creative force, symbolized in ancient times by the oxen that were used for transportation and agriculture. In the mythologies of several cultures, the bull was an emblem of the Creator, the primary deity who provided food for humanity. The letter Aleph also resembles the ancient emblem of the gammadian or fylfot cross, a symbol that appears in virtually all ancient world mythologies as a token of the whirling or rotating energies to be found at the birth of the universe.

The Eleventh Path represents pure potential, not yet set into action. It is potential in search of first experience. The student on the path of Aleph must learn to have complete trust in the Divine, which cannot be comprehended.

CHAPTER FIVE

A TREE WALK WITH THE PATHS

The twenty-two Paths that connect the ten Sephiroth can also be used to expand on the original Tree Walk given in Chapter One. The result will be a more comprehensive version of the Tree Walk, which will give the audience a broader understanding of the *Nativoth*.

The fundamental form of the drama remains the same, so there is no need for us to repeat the speeches of the Sephirotic guides. However, the following stage instructions and speeches can easily be inserted into the basic script.

Only three additional actors will have to be chosen to represent the paths, although the number of path guides needed at any given time varies from one to three. They should wear plain robes in the various colors of the paths, or to simplify things, they may all dress in one color, so long as that color is not exactly the same as any those worn by the Sephirotic guides. Large Hebrew letters symbolizing the paths should be the only symbols used by the path guides. These may be glued on simple collars made of ribbon or string, or better yet, they may be attached to the front of the robes using Velcro, so that they can be quickly attached or removed.

During the speeches of the Sephirotic guides, the path guides should position themselves in a row between the Sephirotic guide giving the speech and the next Sephirah. After the speech, the Hermit leads the Tree Walkers to the path guides, who briefly explain their nature and functions. Then the Hermit may ask the Tree Walkers what path should be chosen to continue the journey. No matter what the audience chooses, the Hermit should persuade them to take the path that leads directly from the last Sephirah to the next in the natural order on the Tree of Life.

This variation also calls for an actor to play the guide of Daath, situated somewhere in the middle of the four stations of Chokmah, Binah, Chesed, and Geburah. The guide of Daath should not wear any symbols, but may be robed and veiled in lavender or light gray.

THE PATH STATIONS

After Malkuth

Number of Path Guides: 1

Path Number: 32

Props: A blue-violet or plain-colored robe. Hebrew letter Tau

The Address of the 32nd Path

"I am the path that leads from Malkuth to Yesod. I am Tau. I am marked with the sign of the Cross. I am the Cross-road. I am the Administrative Intelligence. I govern the movement of all the celestial bodies—the planets and stars that are around you and within you. All in their own proper courses.

"I am a deep dark cavern that reaches into the underworld, into the inner recesses of your own mind. If you fear me, you only fear yourself. I am your first taste of what lies beyond the five senses. I can take you anywhere in this universe. I am your first step unto the path of the mystic. I am the end, and I am just beginning."

(Hermit and Tree Walkers follow the 32nd Path guide to Yesod.)

After Yesod

Number of Path Guides: 2

Path Numbers: 31 and 30

Props: *For Path 31:* A red or plain-colored robe.
Hebrew letter Shin.

> *For Path 30:* An orange or plain-colored robe.
> Hebrew letter Resh.

The Address of the 31st Path

"I am the path that leads from Malkuth to Hod. I am Shin. I am the piecing tooth of the flame. I am the fire of creation. I am the Perpetual Intelligence. I regulate the motions of the Sun and Moon—the archetypal male and female energies within. I separate, purify, and recombine these powers into a greater unity. And this is a constant process that requires perpetual awareness and care. My fires must never be left unattended.

"I am the hidden flame. The secret fire of manifestation. I am the connection between your body and your mind. Hear me, and know that you are not alone. See me, and begin the alchemical process. Touch me, and feel the purification of the flame. Know me, and you will be reborn as the phoenix."

The Address of the 30th Path

"I am the path that leads from Yesod to Hod. I am Resh. I am the head, which gives wisdom. I am the face that you seek to see. I am the Collecting Intelligence. I collect all thoughts and allocate them to a higher purpose. I have established the laws of the universe so that there may be order and stability.

"I am the giver of increase, expansion, and growth. When I analyze the universe, all its splendors are revealed. My thoughts give you increased awareness of the Divine. My thoughts heal your wounds of separateness. I am consciousness, both divine and human. When your face is turned toward my face, you will discover that we two are one."

(Hermit and Tree Walkers follow the 30th Path guide to Hod.)

After Hod

Number of Path Guides: 3

Path Numbers: 29, 28, and 27

Props: For Path 29: A red-violet or plain-colored robe. Hebrew letter Qoph.

For Path 28: A violet or plain-colored robe. Hebrew letter Tzaddi.

For Path 27: A red or plain-colored robe. Hebrew letter Peh.

The Address of the 29th Path

"I am the path that leads from Malkuth to Netzach. I am Qoph. I am the back of the head. I am hidden behind the face of the Creator. I am the Corporeal Intelligence. I form the body of all worlds. I am the reproducer of worlds. I am the procreator. Understand that mind and body are two sides of the same being.

"I am intuition. I am imagination. I am the consciousness that exists within the cells of your body. In dreaming, you may find me. I am the great unknown—the underground river of your subconscious mind. Look into my waters and you can see both heaven and hell. The vision is yours to choose."

The Address of the 28th Path

"I am the path that leads from Yesod to Netzach. I am Tzaddi. I am the hook that catches the fish. I am the sharp seeker in the dark waters of the subconscious. I am the Natural Intelligence. All things in the universe, whether known or unknown, are perfect and natural.

"I am meditation and focused contemplation. I am the human, meditating on the Divine. I am the Divine, meditating on the human. I seek to know, and I seek to be known. Patiently I await those moments of crystal clarity, when all is revealed in a flood of illumination. For these are the moments when the creation of the universe continues."

The Address of the 27th Path

"I am the path that leads from Hod to Netzach. I am Peh. I am the mouth that speaks the word of creation. I am the word of power. I am the Exciting Intelligence. I energize all beings with movement. I infuse all beings with spirit.

"I am also the balance between emotion and intellect. I am the power of vibration. I am that which holds molecules together, and also that which splits them apart. I am the creator and the destroyer. For what is creation, if not the destruction of what existed before? I break down the old to make way for the new. I am the renewer of life. If you fear me, you only fear the natural process of change."

(Hermit and Tree Walkers follow the 27th Path guide to Netzach.)

After Hod

Number of Path Guides: 3

Path Numbers: 26, 25, and 24

Props: For Path 26: A blue-violet or plain-colored robe. Hebrew letter Ayin.

For Path 25: A blue or plain-colored robe. Hebrew letter Samekh.

For Path 24: A blue-green or plain-colored robe. Hebrew letter Nun.

The Address of the 26th Path

"I am the path that leads from Hod to Tiphareth. I am Ayin, the all-seeing eye. I distinguish between truth and illusion. I am the Renewing Intelligence. I am the birth canal for the divine life-force. I renew and rejuvenate all things in the universe.

"I am the master of matter and form. Human minds are formed in the image of matter. This is a limitation to be overcome. Surrender the outer vision for the inner.

"I am the reproducer of physical form. But do not let the appearance of that form lead you into deception. Look beyond illusionary appearances with the inner eye that never blinks, and can never be deceived. Look beyond all images to see the beauty of Tiphareth."

The Address of the 25th Path

"I am the path that leads from Yesod to Tiphareth. I am Samekh. I am that which pushes you to the limits of your endurance. I am also that which supports you when your endurance is waning. I am the Intelligence of Probation. I am the great tempter. I tempt you in order to measure your valor and your merit.

"I constantly test your ability to discriminate between right and wrong. I force you to question your spiritual beliefs, so that you may know those beliefs that are truly yours from mere dogma that you have learned to repeat like a parrot. Sun and Moon, fire and water must be balanced within your soul. Trial and error are my gifts to you. But these are the props that help you to learn wisdom. For you must be tempered like a study sword—forged in the fire and water—in order to be fit and worthy for the spiritual quest."

The Address of the 24th Path

"I am the path that leads from Netzach to Tiphareth. I am Nun. I am the fish—the object of your search into the waters of consciousness. I am the image of fertility and new growth. I am the Imaginative Intelligence. Ever creating new images that aid you in your path to spiritual evolution.

"I am the fish that swims in the eternal sea, never ceasing, always changing. My change brings growth. Some call this a path of death. I call it a path of life. You must forgo the wants of the lower for a higher divine love. To the lower self, this is indeed a type of death, but to the higher self, it is the beginning of new life. Many fear to tread this path, because they fear to let the old ways die and make way for the birth of the new. If they but knew the illumination that I bring, they would not hesitate to make the journey. Mine is the hidden knowledge that is too dazzling to be seen with mortal sight. My gift is immortality. It is a gift given only to the wise."

(Hermit and Tree Walkers follow the 24th Path guide to Tiphareth.)

After Tiphareth

Number of Path Guides: 2

Path Numbers: 23 and 22

Props: For Path 23: A blue or plain-colored robe.
Hebrew letter Mem.

For Path 22: A green or plain-colored robe.
Hebrew letter Lamed.

The Address of the 23rd Path

"I am the path that leads from Hod to Geburah. I am Mem, the waters of creation. I am the mirror that reflects back a reversed image. I am the Stable and Consistent Intelligence. I am the stillness and the fixed purpose. And I have stabilized and calmed the opposing energies of fire and water. And I hold all things in perfect suspension, so that I may gaze into the waters of life and see a reflection of myself.

"I am a symbol of the universal consciousness, the great and endless sea. Immersion into the waters of Mem is baptism into the womb of the universe. It is a cleansing process that dissolves away all that is impure. Complete transformation. Complete mental focus. Suspension of all that went before. Unwavering sacrifice for the higher. Through me you will become the sacred chalice that is a fit vessel for the holy spirit. Those who seek to lose themselves in my deep waters will find themselves. Looking in the waters, they shall see the face of the Divine reflected back unto them."

The Address of the 22nd Path

"I am the path that leads from Tiphareth to Geburah. I am Lamed, the ox-goad—that which prods and guides you to take the correct path and keep you from harm. I keep you from wandering off the chosen road. I am the Faithful Intelligence. All the dwellers of earth are protected under my shadow. And I increase all spiritual virtues of those who remain true to the divine will.

"Force and form. Creation and destruction. Order and chaos. I am the reconciler between them. I am the power of balance, pouring forth the divine life-force in an equilibrating manner, with perfect justice. I am impartial and judicial. I do not play favorites. On this path, you shall receive your just reward. No more and no less. My lessons may seem harsh at times, but they only provide exactly what you need, not what you want. So mote it be."

(Hermit and Tree Walkers follow the 22nd Path guide to Geburah.)

After Geburah

Number of Path Guides: 3

Path Numbers: 21, 20, and 19

Props: For Path 21: A violet or plain-colored robe.
Hebrew letter Kaph.

For Path 20: A yellow-green or plain-colored robe.
Hebrew letter Yod.

For Path 19: A yellow or plain-colored robe.
Hebrew letter Teth.

The Address of the 21st Path

"I am the path that leads from Netzach to Chesed. I am Kaph, the open palm of the hand—the hand of one who reaches for the higher. I am the Intelligence of Conciliation and Reward. I reward and bless those who aspire with dedication to the Great Work.

"Many seek, but few will find me. Many are called but few are chosen. Be strong and diligent, and I may touch the palm of your hand.

"I am the quest revolving upon itself in perfect equilibrium, ever balanced, ever perfect, binding all opposites together. I am the perfect circle of destiny and karma. Rest assured that there is no place in the cosmos where there are such things as deficiency, inequity, or defeat. All images of such things are simply the illusion of isolation. For I am everywhere.

Even in those arcane places that you do not understand. So take care that you do not condemn that which you cannot comprehend. All that is unknown to you contains a lesson.

"I am the desire within you that drives the hunger for the Divine. I am the part of you that searches for meaning and the essence of God. Maintain your balance and the rewards of the heavens shall be within your grasp."

The Address of the 20th Path

"I am the path that leads from Tiphareth to Chesed. I am Yod, the hand of the one who reaches down to assist you. The hand of the universal architect. I am the Intelligence of Will. I prepare all created beings by introducing them to the will and wisdom of the Divine. In your prayers and meditations, and in the solitude of your mind, you will come to understand me.

"I am the point of beginning, the spark of creation, self-generated. I am the circle of union. My power commences all motion. My essence gives all things substance. My wisdom is the basis of all knowledge.

"My gifts belong to the mystic, the prophet, and the master magician. My path must be trodden alone. My initiates travel unaided—except for the aid that I myself provide. And after you have attained my wisdom, remember the hand that helped you—and extend your hand to help another."

The Address of the 19th Path

"I am the path that leads from Geburah to Chesed. I am Teth, the guiding serpent—the Serpent of Wisdom. I am the Intelligence of the Secret spiritual activities. I bestow the ineffable secrets of number, names, vibration, and expansion.

"I am hidden from the uninitiated. But the mystic and the magician know me well. I am energy, fiery and fluid. I sit between fire and water, severity and mercy. Their combined energies generate my power. I am the serpent of the Garden of Eden and the Brazen Serpent of the Moses. I am the tempter and that which overcomes temptation. I am the healer and the redeemer. I am the tamer of the wild beast. I am the knower of secrets. I know the holy name that no one may speak.

"Too much severity is cruelty and oppression. Too much mercy is but weakness and the fading out of the will. Within these simple statements are profound mysteries. Those who come to understand secret and divine things will have fortitude. I will empower them and give them great strength and the will to use it wisely."

(Hermit and Tree Walkers follow the 19th Path guide to Chesed.)

After Chesed

Number of Path Guides: 2

Path Numbers: 18 and 17

Props: *For Path 18*: A yellow-orange or plain-colored robe. Hebrew letter Cheth.

For Path 17: An orange or plain-colored robe. Hebrew letter Zayin.

The Address of the 18th Path

"I am the path that leads from Geburah to Binah. I am Cheth, the protecting enclosure. I am the fence as well as all that is enclosed by it. I am the Intelligence or House of Influence. I lavish goodness from the Divine upon those who dwell under the protection of my wings in the realm of manifestation. I protect you from the brilliant darkness and the light-filled night. For you cannot look upon it and live.

"I am hidden from your conscious mind. Your language means nothing to me. I cannot use it. I speak instead to the larger portion of your mind, your subconscious self. I organize energy into symbolic form that your deep self understands well.

"I contain and divide energy into its various forms so that you may learn about it and grow in your knowledge. But do not mistake these divisions of reality for reality itself. For they are merely a convenience designed for your education. And like all school books, you will one day outgrow the need for them.

"Never forget that you are the Cheth, the enclosure for the divine spirit that dwells within you. And some day when your spirit has grown in its knowledge, it will have no need of boundaries."

The Address of the 17th Path

"I am the path that leads from Tiphareth to Binah. I am Zayin, the sword. I am that which cuts the divine life force into separate parts as it continues down the Tree. This is self-reflection, creation through division. I am the Disposing Intelligence. I prepare the righteous for the final part of their ascent. Those who would walk my path must be fit, balanced, and strong. They must be clothed with the holy spirit. For I am the path that brings the sacrificed son back to the womb of the mother.

"My sword divides my oneness into many forms. Those who would climb the Tree by way of my path must reverse the process of separation. You are already separated, so in your ascent, you must unite and become whole again. Put duality to the sword. See the cuts of division disappear as I become one again. Thus will you come to know my undivided love. It is the love between mother and child who are but one being."

After the 17th Path

(The Hermit explains the following to the Tree Walkers:)

"Fellow travelers, we are approaching the realm of the Supernals at the top of the Tree of Life. But there is no straight path of ascent from the fourth Sephirah of Chesed to the third Sephirah of Binah. Why is this? I will summarize it in a parable:

"After the creation of the universe, the earth was a savage but beautiful paradise, a Garden of Eden where mankind existed as one of the animals in nature. For the Elohim created the universe of humankind after their likeness. But humans tasted fruit from the Tree of the Knowledge of Good and of Evil. That is to say, they became sentient beings, the only creatures in the manifest universe with the awesome power to use thought and willpower to advance either good or evil in the world. Thus were they separated from other creatures. The race of humankind was too young and naive to control this terrible power of knowledge. Not only did they become separated from the other creatures in the garden, but they separated all things within their own minds—reason from intuition, animus from anima, soul from spirit, and human from divine. Thus did they become unbalanced and distracted from the Divine.

"And the unbalanced portion of humanity's psyche began to threaten to overtake the influence of the holy Sephiroth within it. So Tetragrammaton Elohim placed the four letters YHVH of the equilibrated name and the Flaming Sword of the ten Sephiroth between the devastated garden and the Supernal Eden, that this portion should not be involved in humanity's imbalance. A fracture appeared in the Tree—a great abyss that separated the Supernals from the lower parts of the Tree. And a hole appeared in the position of Daath, where once there had been a Sephirah. Now no path leads directly across the abyss from Chesed to Binah. And the great task for humanity is to figure out a way for each person to re-establish that connecting link to the Supernals and restore the Tree of Life within. In this is a great mystery that each of you must solve alone. For I can do no more than guide you on this journey. But for now, take my hand and we shall try to find our way across the abyss."

(The Tree Walkers grasp hands, with the Hermit in the forefront. The Hermit leads the line of Tree Walkers in a great spiral—eventually circling inward to the station of Daath. They continue to grasp hands and slowly circle the Guide of Daath as he or she addresses them. The guide is rather ghost-like, and somewhat detached—not seeming to take much notice of the Tree Walkers.)

The Address of Daath

"Reverse all knowledge. Knowledge all reverse. The Head which is not a head. The Tree whose roots are above its branches. What is below? What is above? Dissolve. Dissolve. Dissolve. Cast away all you have learned. Remember what is forgotten. The sleeper must awaken."

(The guide of Daath repeats these same lines over and over again, three times or more. The Hermit leads the Tree Walkers away, while the guide is still speaking. The Hermit spirals the Walkers outward until they arrive at the station of Binah.)

After Binah

Number of Path Guides: 3

Path Numbers: 16, 15, and 14

Props: For Path 16: A red-orange or plain-colored robe. Hebrew letter Vav.

For Path 15: A red or plain-colored robe. Hebrew letter Heh.

For Path 14: A green or plain-colored robe. Hebrew letter Daleth.

The Address of the 16th Path

"I am the path that leads from Chesed to Chokmah. I am Vav, the nail that attaches, the pin that connects. I am the Triumphal or Eternal Intelligence. I am the pleasure of merciful Chesed, receiving harmony from the wisdom above. I prepare the paradise that awaits all true seekers.

"Mine is an exalted path of high attainment. Only those who are well disciplined and virtuous can find this route. I am unity—I connect that which is above to that which is below. I am the link between the worlds. All is joined together through me. My gift is great wisdom. But you must listen in order to hear it. Be still and listen.

"My voice is within you. I am the expounder of the mysteries. I am your mentor. I am the only teacher you have ever had. All the books you have ever read were written by me. Know that I am, and always will be, your initiator."

The Address of the 15th Path

"I am the path that leads from Tiphareth to Chesed. I am Heh, the window to the heavens. I am the portal for the divine breath of wisdom. I am life. I am being. I am the Constituting Intelligence. I established the world of divine light and life from the dark womb of the limitless. I bring order to the chaotic. I create cosmic law where there was none. Through me is created the very structure, shape, and support of the Tree of Life.

"I give the power of sight. I see all things as they truly are. I use my sight to define all. Nothing is hidden from me. My gift is sight. So be watchful and attentive for divine things. Use my path as a telescope through which you can see with inner vision. Gaze up, like a son gazes up at his father.

"I am essence, idea, and form. I am merciful and understanding. Know that I am always with you, giving form and stability to your life—and giving you the choice to control your own destiny."

The Address of the 14th Path

"I am the path that leads from Binah to Chokmah. I am Daleth, the door of initiation. I am perfect, brilliant fecundity. I am the Illuminating Intelligence. I am that brilliant flame which prepares the divine life force for conception and birth into manifestation. I am the foundation of the mysteries of the origins of life. I am the womb of creation and the energy link between the Supernal mother and father. I am the archetype of the nuclear family. I am unity, perfect and complete.

"Mine is the path of fertility. I channel force into form. I take on substance. I am the volatile that becomes fixed, the shadow that becomes a body, the spirit that becomes a soul, and the dream that becomes a thought. I produce the various mental images from the Divine which give life to all created beings. Life pours through me on its way to final form. I give limitation to the unlimited. I give manifestation to the unmanifest, that it gaze upon itself in joy and understanding.

"My gifts are imagination and consciousness. Use them creatively in your quest and my door will open to ever higher states of awareness."

(Hermit and Tree Walkers follow the 14th Path guide to Chokmah.)

After Chokmah

Number of Path Guides: 3

Path Numbers: 13, 12, and 11

Props: For Path 13: A blue or plain-colored robe. Hebrew letter Gimel.

For Path 12: A yellow or plain-colored robe. Hebrew letter Beth.

For Path 11: A yellow or plain-colored robe. Hebrew letter Aleph.

The Address of the 13th Path

"I am the path that leads from Tiphareth to Kether. I am Gimel, the camel. The ship of the desert. I am the Uniting Intelligence. I am the direct pathway of the soul on its way back to the Divine. I am the eternal love of the spirit for its soul. I am the clarification and consummation of the sacred truth.

"I am the root-essence of consciousness. I am all-knowing. I am the waters of the subconscious at their purest state flowing directly from the source of Kether. Wave after wave of pure light, flowing in cycles ever downward. I unite all forms of consciousness. All things are touches by my waters. Ever virgin, I remain untouched and unchanged by all that my essence touches. Nothing can debase me. Nothing can erase me.

"Long is the journey on my path. Seemingly endless at times. When you are in the midst of the quest, treading the infinite sand of the desert in search of me, do not think that your task is futile, or that you shall never reach the goal. In such moments, reflect upon me, for I am with you always. I am closer than you suspect. And I await your final initiation."

The Address of the 12th Path

"I am the path that leads from Binah to Kether. I am Beth, the house, the dwelling place of the Divine. I am the Intelligence of Transparency. I am the one who bestows clarity of psychic vision. I am the source of prophecy and revelation. I govern the hidden workings of all dimensions. The highest visions and oracles are under my stewardship. I am the revelation of the divine self as it emerges from the unmanifest. I am the supreme prophet.

"I will, therefore I am. I am the essence of will and of mind. I am the divine will to act, to dare, and to express myself. I am the spirit breath of Eternal that moved upon the face of the waters. I am pure potential in its first action. I am the first action of energy rushing forth to be limited by form in order to manifest myself. All things in the universe were created by my will to see myself reflected into many forms which I continually contemplate. The focus of my contemplation is the breath that gives substance to all created things.

"My gifts are clairvoyance and all types of psychic awareness. These must be wisely used and always dedicated to the highest. Do not dishonor them with low purpose, lest my transparent vision become clouded and opaque."

The Address of the 11th Path

"I am the path that leads from Chokmah to Kether. I am Aleph, the strong ox, the carrier of all burdens. The symbol of the Creator. The primal force. I am the Scintillating Intelligence. I am that shimmering light that broke forth from the darkness of night. I am the curtain that shields the brilliance of the blinding divine light—the veil before the Holy of Holies. I am a buffer of protection between you and the incinerating glory of the light. I alone stand before the Face of the Cause of Causes, that none living may see.

"I am the first and the last. The Alpha and the Omega. The Aleph and the Tau. I am older than the most ancient star. I am younger than a newborn's first breath. I am one perfect, one eternal, one complete. I am all that there is. What are time and space but foolish words to me? I carry the seeds of many. I am pure potential, and I am just beginning in my descent.

"What I am, you cannot understand. Know this: I am that I am. There is nothing else. And at the end of all time, I shall still be."

(The Hermit leads the Tree Walkers, one at a time, following the 11th Path guide to Kether.)

Endnotes

1. From the Portal Ritual as published in Israel Regardie's *The Golden Dawn.*

CHAPTER SIX

THE TREE WITHIN US

The Tree of Life is not just a symbol of "what is out there"—it is also a symbol of "what's in here." This Tree lies at the heart and core of every one of us. The glyph of the Tree can be said to resemble the human body. The Tree of the Greater Universe (the Macrocosm) is often represented in the colossal form of *Adam Kadmon*, or the Archetypal Man. This is an anthropomorphic image of the Divine. The Tree of the Lesser Universe (the Microcosm) is a smaller reflection of Adam Kadmon that exists within all human beings. By working with the Microcosmic Tree within our own souls, we have a direct conduit to its Macrocosmic twin. Through it, we are provided the means for bringing the divine and vitalizing energies of the Sephiroth into our conscious grasp, where they can be grounded into action, and used for many purposes.

How do we bring these energies into our lives? By *will power, visualization,* and *vibration.* Magicians believe that conscious thoughts have their own reality and that human will power is a real, tangible force that is capable of having an impact on the physical universe. By using one's thoughts constructively and focusing them at a specific spiritual level of working, the student can influence the energy patterns that make up the manifest universe. The mind can become a lens through which the projected thought, propelled by will power, is magnified. By discovering how to focus one's thoughts on the images associated with the Kabbalistic Tree of Life and by envisioning oneself *as* the Tree, the student can elevate his or her level of consciousness and convey these Sephirotic powers into daily life. (See Figure 18.)

The Importance of Vibration

Certain deity names that are associated with the Sephiroth attract these Qabalisitc energies when they are properly intoned or vibrated. One of the reasons ancient names of the deity are used rather than more modern versions is because of the fact that spiritual seekers have been using these same names, linking their energy to them through centuries of living ritual work. But even more importantly, because the words themselves are *sacred words* that are connected to the divine powers that they represent. *"By names*

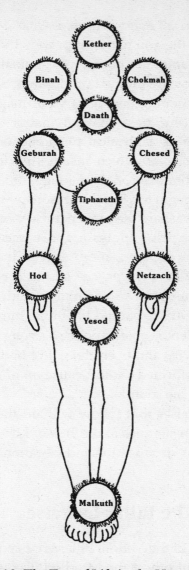

Figure 18: The Tree of Life in the Human Body

and Images are all Powers Awakened and Re-awakened."
Vibration of the god name empowers the word.

Divine names are not simply spoken in spiritual exercises, they are intoned or vibrated. Scientists are only now becoming aware of what magicians have known for centuries—that all matter is vibratory energy. There is a physical phenomenon known as *harmonic resonance,* which means that if one object starts to vibrate strongly enough, another object nearby will begin to vibrate or resonate with the first, if both objects share the same natural vibratory rate.

The Kabbalist vibrates a god name in order to effect a harmonic resonance between the deity as it exists within his own psyche and as it exists within the greater universe. To vibrate a god name takes practice. The name should be intoned in such a way that the student is able to notice a strong vibration in the chest cavity and even the entire body. Vibration properly performed should cause all of existence to vibrate with the sound.

The exercises that follow will aid the student in activating the energies of the Tree of Life through the techniques of visualization and vibration.

The Middle Pillar Exercise

The exercise of the Middle Pillar is designed to establish the Sephiroth of the Middle Pillar (the Pillar of Balance) within the aura of the person performing it (see Figure 19). It brings a sense of balance, harmony,

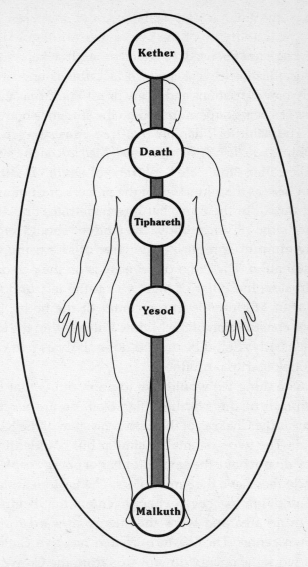

Figure 19: The Spheres of the Middle Pillar

and protection. It also stabilizes and increases the energy and vitality of the person performing it. This exercise can be used to gain strength when one's energy has been weakened. In fact, this is one ritual with many variations and many uses.[1] The Tree is visualized as being superimposed on the student's body.

The Middle Pillar on the Tree consists of four Sephiroth: *Kether, Tiphareth, Yesod, Malkuth,* along with the so-called "invisible Sephirah" of *Daath.*[2] Daath is used here as a conjunction of the powers of Chokmah and Binah. In the aura that interpenetrates and surrounds the physical body, the student should regularly build up a replica of the Tree of Life using the imagination. The Pillar of Severity is on the person's right side, the Pillar of Mercy is on the left, and the Pillar of Mildness is in the center of the body. The astral construction of the Middle Pillar within the student's body should be practiced regularly as part of a life-long spiritual routine.

One thing we would like to point out is that the Sephiroth of the Middle Pillar Exercise are *not* the same as the Chakras of the Eastern system of the Kundalini. The two systems are similar but not identical. They do not have the same number of energy centers, nor do they have the same colors. The Eastern system of Kundalini has seven energy centers that begin in the groin area and work the energy upward to the Crown center. The Western system has five centers that work the energy downwards from the Crown to the feet. Many writers make the mistake of calling the Sephiroth "chakras." This often causes confusion. It would be more appropriate to refer to the Sephiroth of the Middle Pillar as "centers," "spheres," "Sephiroth" or *"galgals"* (which is Hebrew for "whirlings").

The Middle Pillar Exercise

This exercise can be performed either standing, sitting, or lying down. After a few minutes of relaxation, imagine a sphere of white light just above your head. Vibrate the name **"EHEIEH"** (Eh-hey-yah), meaning "I am." Keep vibrating this word until it is the only thought in your conscious mind. Maintain a strong visualization of the sphere. Then imagine a shaft of light descending from your Kether center to your Daath center at the nape of the neck.

Form a sphere of light at the Daath center. Vibrate the name **"YHVH ELOHIM"** (Yode-heh-vav-heh El-oh-heem), meaning "the Lord God." Intone the name until it is the only thing in your conscious mind. The sphere is strongly visualized.

Bring a shaft of light down from the Daath center to the Tiphareth center around the area of your heart. Form a sphere of light there. Vibrate the name **"YHVH ELOAH VE-DAATH"** (Yode-heh-vav-heh El-oh-ah V'-Dah-ath), meaning "Lord God of Knowledge," several times until it fills your consciousness. See the sphere strongly in your mind's eye.

See the shaft of light descending from Tiphareth into the Yesod center in the genital region. Imagine a sphere of light formed there. Intone the name

"SHADDAI EL CHAI" (Shah-dye El-Chai), meaning "Almighty Living God," several times as before. The image of the sphere becomes stronger.

Visualize the shaft of light descending from Yesod into your Malkuth center at the feet and ankles. Vibrate the name **"ADONAI HA-ARETZ"** (Ah-doe-nye Ha-Ah-retz), meaning "Lord of Earth," a number of times as before. See the sphere clearly in your mind.

Imagine the Middle Pillar complete. Then circulate the light you have brought down through the Middle Pillar around the outside of your body to strengthen your aura. Using the cycles of breathing, bring the light up one side of the body and down the other, from Malkuth to Kether and back again. Bring the light up the left side and down the right. After performing this for a short period of time, imagine the ribbon of light descending down the front of your body and rising up your back.

Still employing rhythmic breathing, visualize the shaft of light rising up the Middle Pillar in the center of your body. When it reaches Kether, imagine a shower of light surrounding the outside of your body as it descends to Malkuth again. Circulate the light in this manner for some time. Then see the light rise again in a ribbon that spirals around the outside of your body.

Finally focus some of the energy back into your Tiphareth center, the seat of equilibrium and balance.

Appendix to the Middle Pillar

You may decide to end the exercise with the Kabbalistic Cross to indicate that you have called down the light of your Kether and balanced it within your aura. Then let your imagination dwell on the aura and see it oval and clear, pulsating with the glow from Tiphareth.

Although it is not a part of the traditional Middle Pillar exercise, we like to finish the rite by vibrating the divine names, **"YEHESHUAH, YEHOVASHAH"** (Yeh-heh-shu-ah, Yeh-hoh-vah-shah). This is the Pentagrammaton or *Five-Lettered Name of God.* Interpreted by the Christians as the Hebrew name of Jesus, it actually represents the Tetragrammaton or Four-Lettered Name of God (*YHVH,* which encompasses the four elements of Fire, Water, Air, and Earth) with the fifth Element of Spirit in the middle of the four letters. Spirit is represented by the Hebrew letter Shin. Thus the Pentagrammaton or Yeheshuah is transliterated in Hebrew as *YHShVH.*

Uses of the Middle Pillar

The exercise of the Middle Pillar will help to cleanse, soothe, and balance the aura. It can be performed as a preparation for meditation. When you have practiced the exercise of the Middle Pillar for some time and can visualize easily, you can establish the other Sephiroth within your aura by vibrating the deity names (see the Archangelic Middle Pillar).

If you are called to see anyone who is ill, depressed, or who has a depressing effect on you, you should perform this exercise beforehand. You may also imagine that your aura is hardened at the edge, so that a person is unable to penetrate it, and deplete you of vitality.

It is better at first to keep your aura to yourself, rather than try to flow out towards others. Unless you are particularly vital and well balanced, you will only waste energy. Modes of healing should be tabled for the time being. Such methods have a technique of their own and require trained and balanced minds and bodies to carry them out. The student is advised to "get right" with him/her self before interfering in any way with others.

A Simplified Middle Pillar

Instead of using the divine Hebrew names, the beginner may opt to use the following words in English. When the concepts of the Sephiroth as suggested by these words become more familiar, they may be replaced with the more traditional names.

Top of Head	*(Kether)*	**"Spirit,"**
Throat	*(Daath)*	**"Knowledge,"**
Heart	*(Tiphareth)*	**"Love,"**
Groin	*(Yesod)*	**"Creation,"**
Feet	*(Malkuth)*	**"Matter,"**
Center	*(seat of balance)*	**"Unity, All Is One."**

Working with Archangels

Each Sephirah is assigned an archangel and a group of angels (sometimes called a "choir" of angels. An *angel* is a pure and high spirit of unmixed good in office and operation. In the Kabbalah, angels and archangels are considered specific aspects of God, each with a particular purpose and jurisdiction. They are anthropomorphic symbols of what we believe to be good or holy. Nearly all of the Hebrew angels have the suffixes "el" or "yah" at the end of their names, alluding that they are "of God."

Powerful angels that govern large groups of lesser angels are known as archangels. Archangels are intelligent beings that carry out the divine will in each Sephirah. They each govern the lower forces that exist within each Sephirah—mediating between higher and lower forms of energy, and they also have specific duties that relate to the Sephirah that they are assigned to. Archangels symbolize intelligent forces in nature that are responsible for making certain that the "machinery" of the universe is in working order on all levels.

Angels occupy the realms that are between the Godhead and humanity. They are intermediaries who relay information to us from the deity. They intercede on our behalf as we turn our attention to the divine, opening up channels of communication between the different levels of consciousness.

Employing the archangels and angels is a more personal way to approach the Tree of Life. This is because the higher divine names cannot be represented in human form—the way the archangels can. Although these beings in reality are probably better represented as geometric shapes or great pillars of light, they certainly can and do present themselves to us in human shape. They also exist in levels that are somewhat closer to our own physical plane. The energy of the angels is denser than that of the Godhead, but not as dense as the energy of the physical world.

Angels and archangels are intelligent, compassionate, individual, and earnest. Working with them in meditations and exercises such as the Middle Pillar provides the student with a gracious source of wisdom and divine love.

The Archangelic Middle Pillar
An Advanced Exercise

Close your eyes and begin a cycle of rhythmic breathing. Breathe deeply. Imagine a white enclosed flower bud above the crown of your head. It is a flower waiting to be born. You are going to awaken this flower by vibrating three times the Divine name of Kether, which is **EHEIEH** (Eh-heh-yah). As you vibrate, the flower will stir into life. The bud opens to reveal a large brilliant white lotus flower. Kether is activated.

Now vibrate three times the name of the Archangel of Kether which is **Metatron** (Meh-tah-tron). See the flower petals of the lotus become as great white angelic wings. The petals of the lotus grow larger in size until they become the wings of an enormous Archangel whose form envelopes you like a mighty cloak.

This is **Metatron,** the Archangel of Kether, dressed in robes of brilliant white. He is a mighty masculine form with thick dark curly hair and beard. Two rays of light crown his head on either side. His face is reflective and dreamlike. His body is strong, large and fiery. His feet also are winged.

The Hebrew name **Metatron** has no clear etymological base and may in fact be a "channeled" name. Some have tried to provide a Greek etymological base for it, and have translated the name as *meta ton thronos* or "near Thy throne." He is described as the Angel of the Presence and the World Prince. Metatron alone sees the Eternal One face to face. He presides over the whole Tree of Life as well as Kether, and is considered the right-hand masculine Kerub of the Ark of the Covenant. Tradition has it that Metatron communicated the Kabbalah to humankind. He has the additional titles of "The Lesser YHVH," the "King of Angels," "the Great Scribe," and the name **IOEL**— which means "I am God." Metatron is responsible for presenting God and human being to each other. He is the link between humans and the Divine. See him.

Next, imagine a gray-white enclosed flower bud at the area of your throat. It is another lotus of knowledge waiting to be awakened. You are going to animate this flower by vibrating three times the divine name of Daath, which is **YHVH ELOHIM** (Yode-heh-vav-heh

El-oh-heem). As you vibrate, the flower will stir into life. The bud opens to reveal a beautiful large brilliant gray-white lotus flower. Daath is activated.

Now vibrate three times the name of the archangel associated with Daath, which is **Tzaphqiel** (Tzaf-kee-el). As you do so, the flower petals of the lotus will become like great gray-white (almost silvery) angelic wings. The petals of the lotus grow larger in size until they become the wings of an enormous Archangel whose figure surrounds you like a cape.

This is **Tzaphqiel**, the archangel of Binah and Daath, dressed in robes of gray-white. She is slender and well proportioned, with dark hair framing a thoughtful, intellectual face. Her delicate white skin disguises her great strength and determination. At her feet are the symbols of justice: the sword and the scales of Libra.

Her name, **Tzaphqiel**, means "Beholder of God." She is the Eye of God, watching and observing, through which the Divine knows all and sees all. Tzaphqiel governs meditation and contemplation. She is the archangel of the divine temple. She is behind the formation of all mystical groups that have been formed by non-physical teachers or illuminated masters who have evolved beyond the need for a human body. She assists these masters to teach those of us who are less evolved. Tzaphqiel is also the archangel of Primal Manifestation. See her.

Next, imagine a golden-yellow flower bud in the middle of your being at the center of your heart. It is a lotus still in the womb. You are going to awaken this flower by vibrating three times the divine name of Tiphareth, which is **YHVH ELOAH VE-DAATH** (Yode-heh-vav-heh El-oh-ah V'-Dah-ath). As you vibrate, the bud will transform into a flower. The bud unfolds to reveal a large brilliant golden yellow lotus flower. Tiphareth is aroused.

We will now vibrate three times the name of the archangel of Tiphareth which is **Raphael** (Rah-fah-el). As you do so, the flower petals of the lotus become as great golden angelic wings. The petals of the lotus grow larger in size until they become the wings of an enormous Archangel whose form envelopes you like a garment of light.

This is **Raphael,** the archangel of Tiphareth, dressed in robes of gold trimmed with violet. He is a strong masculine form with a youthful face framed by fine blond hair. His face shows great strength and determination, but also tranquillity and kindness. His feet are winged and he holds the Caduceus Wand of Hermes.

His name, **Raphael,** means "Healer of God," or "God has healed." Raphael is the archangel specially appointed to heal the wounds (both physical and spiritual) of humankind. He is the archangel attributed to the powers of the divine intellect. Raphael is a teacher of the Hermetic Arts, thus pointing to his association with Tiphareth, the sphere of healing whose divine name means "Lord God of Knowledge." See him.

Next, a rich violet flower bud in the area of your groin. It is a flower waiting to come to life. You are going to energize this flower by vibrating three times the divine name of Yesod, which is **SHADDAI EL CHAI** (Shah-dye El-Chai). As you vibrate, the bud will transform into a flower. The bud unfolds to reveal a large luscious lotus flower. Yesod is awakened.

Now vibrate three times the name of the archangel of Yesod which is **Gabriel** (Gah-bree-el). As you do so, the flower petals of the lotus become as great violet angelic wings. The petals of the lotus grow larger in size until they become the wings of an enormous Archangel whose figure envelopes you like a mighty cloak.

This is **Gabriel**, the archangel of Yesod, dressed in robes of violet trimmed with yellow and blue. She has a full beautiful face and body which displays a sense of pride and dominance. She is active and changeable, and her feet are also winged. Her symbol on the Tree is the horn or trumpet.

Her name, **Gabriel,** means "The Strong One of God," or "the Strength of God." She is the Archangel of the Annunciation and the Resurrection. Gabriel is the Divine messenger who relays information between the Divine Creator and humanity as a whole. She gives us the powers of vision and hearing, as well as the powers of life and procreation. See her.

Next, imagine a multi-colored flower bud at your feet and ankles. It is a flower awaiting rebirth. You are going to awaken this flower by vibrating three times the Divine name of Malkuth, which is **ADONAI HA-ARETZ** (Ah-doe-nye Ha-Ah-retz). As you vibrate, the flower will stir into life. The bud opens to reveal a large lotus flower in the colors of citrine, russet brown, olive green and deep black. Malkuth is activated.

We will now vibrate three times the name of the archangel of Malkuth, which is **Sandalphon** (San-dahl-fon). You see the flower petals of the lotus become as great angelic wings. The petals of the lotus grow larger in size until they become the wings of an enormous archangel whose form envelopes you like a great cape.

This is **SANDALPHON,** the archangel of Malkuth, dressed in robes of the Malkuth colors. She is a great tall feminine archangel with dark hair ornamented with grape leaves and vines. Two rays of light crown her head on either side. Her face is beautiful and compassionate. Her body is full and strong. Her feet are also winged.

Her Hebrew name has no clear etymological base and may in fact be a "channeled" name. Some have tried to provide a Greek etymological base for it, and have translated the name variously as "co-brother," "Lord of the extent of Height," or "the sound of sandals." Sandalphon is the twin of Metatron, and is in fact considered another form of Metatron, although feminine. This points to the idea that Malkuth is the same as Kether, but after another manner. Sandalphon is the archangel of the Earth sphere. She is also the left-hand feminine Kerub of the Ark of the Covenant. Her duty is to mediate and sort out material energies that are to be brought forth into physical manifestation. See her.

At this point you have awakened the archangels of the Middle Pillar within your aura. Imagine all five archangels that we have summoned surrounding you—five great winged beings who are here to protect and teach you. The radiant archangel **Raphael** steps forward to bring you a special gift of healing. In his hands he bears a gift for you. Only you know what this gift looks like. See the gift. Visualize it.

Take the gift and absorb it into your heart center. As you do so, feel its healing warmth radiating throughout your body. You thank the archangel Raphael for this gift. And you also thank the rest of the archangels for their presence and the light they have brought you.

Finally, circulate the energy around your body, strengthening your aura. Use the cycles of breathing: *Exhale*—bring the light from Kether down the left side of your body to Malkuth. *Inhale*—draw the energy up the right side of the body from Malkuth to Kether. Up one side of the body and down the other, from Malkuth to Kether and back again. After performing this for a short period of time, change the direction of the energy. *Exhale*—imagine the ribbon of light going down the front of your body from Kether to Malkuth. *Inhale*—draw the energy up the back of the body from Malkuth to Kether.

Still employing rhythmic breathing, visualize the shaft of light rising up the Middle Pillar in the center of your body. When it reaches Kether, imagine a shower of light surrounding the outside of your body as it descends to Malkuth again. Circulate the light in this manner for some time.

Then see the light rise again in a ribbon that spirals around the outside of your body. Finally focus some of the energy back into your Tiphareth center, the seat of equilibrium and balance. Finish the rite by vibrating one time the divine names, **"YEHESHUAH, YEHO-VASHAH"** (Yeh-heh-shu-ah, Yeh-hoh-vah-shah).

Color Visualization Techniques

One of the many variations of the Middle Pillar Exercise involves the use of color. Color, like vibration, is a potent energy force that has a profound influence on the subconscious mind. By visualizing the Sephiroth of the Tree in the various colors that are associated with them, the student can focus in on and activate these energies in a more precise manner. It is a method for fine-tuning these energies for a specific purpose or need.

There are actually four colors that are associated with each Sephirah. However, only two of these colors are usually employed with any regularity.[3] These are described as the *King Scale* and the *Queen Scale* colors of the Sephiroth. These titles denote masculine and feminine potencies (symbolized by certain colors) that exist within each sphere at all times.

Sephirah	King Scale	Queen Scale
Kether	Brilliant White	White Brilliance
Chokmah	Soft Blue	Gray
Binah	Crimson	Black
(Daath)	(Lavender)	(Gray White)
Chesed	Deep Violet	Blue
Geburah	Orange	Red
Tiphareth	Rose Pink	Yellow
Netzach	Amber	Green
Hod	Violet	Orange
Yesod	Indigo	Violet
Malkuth	Yellow	(Citrine/Russet/Olive/Black)

The King Scale is considered masculine and thus has certain male characteristics attributed to it. It is *stimulating, outgoing,* and *active.* The Queen scale is thought of as feminine, and therefore is regarded as *receptive, open,* and *passive.* Most diagrams of the Tree of Life show the Sephiroth in their Queen Scale colors, because taken as a whole, the Sephiroth are seen as having feminine characteristics—they are open and receptive to the energies that flow into them from the divine source.[4]

The following exercise shows how to arouse and open all of the Sephiroth on the Tree employing color along with vibration.

The Exercise of the Three Pillars

This exercise can also be performed either standing, sitting, or lying down. After a few minutes of relaxation, imagine a sphere of white light just above your head. Vibrate the name **"EHEIEH"** (Eh-hey-yah). Keep vibrating this word until it is the only thought in your conscious mind. Maintain a strong visualization of the white sphere.

Then imagine a shaft of white light descending from your Kether center to your Chokmah center at the left temple of your forehead. Visualize a sphere of gray light there. Intone the name of **"YAH"** (meaning "Lord"). Keep vibrating the name until it is the complete focus of all your attention. Continue to visualize the gray sphere strongly.

Bring a shaft of white light horizontally across from your Chokmah center to your Binah center at the right temple of your forehead. Form a sphere of black light there. Vibrate the name **"YHVH ELOHIM"** (Yode-heh-vav-heh El-oh-heem) a number of times until it occupies all of your mind. Maintain a strong visualization of the black sphere.

Now bring a shaft of white light down diagonally from your Binah center to your Daath center at the nape of your neck. Visualize a sphere of gray-white light there. Vibrate the name **"YHVH ELOHIM."** Intone the name until it is the only thing in your conscious mind. Maintain a strong visualization of the sphere.

Next, visualize a shaft of white light down diagonally from the Daath center to your Chesed center at your left shoulder. Form a sphere of blue light there. Vibrate the name **"EL"** (meaning "God") a number of times until it occupies all of your mind. Continue to visualize the blue sphere strongly.

Bring a shaft of white light horizontally from the Chesed to your Geburah center at your right shoulder. Visualize a sphere of red light there. Vibrate the name **"ELOHIM GIBOR"** (El-oh-heem Ge-boor) (meaning "God of Battles"). Intone the name until it is the only thing in your conscious mind. Maintain a strong visualization of the red sphere.

Now bring a shaft of light diagonally across from Geburah to your Tiphareth center around the area of your heart. Form a sphere of yellow light there. Vibrate the name **"YHVH ELOAH VE-DAATH"** (Yode-heh-vav-heh El-oh-ah V'-Dah-ath) several times until it fills your consciousness. Maintain a strong visualization of the yellow sphere.

Next, visualize a shaft of white light down diagonally from the Tiphareth center to your Netzach center at your left hip. Form a sphere of green light there. Vibrate the name **"YHVH TZABAOTH"** (Yode-heh-vav-heh Tzah-bah-oth) (meaning "Lord of Hosts") a number of times until it occupies all of your mind. Continue to visualize the green sphere strongly.

Bring a shaft of white light horizontally from the Netzach to your Hod center at your right hip. Form a sphere of orange light there. Vibrate the name **"ELOHIM TZABAOTH"** (El-oh-heem Tzah-bah-oth) (meaning "God of Hosts"). Intone the name until it is the only thing in your conscious mind. Maintain a strong visualization of the orange sphere.

Now see the shaft of white light descending diagonally from Hod into the Yesod center in the genital region. Imagine a sphere of violet light formed there. Intone the name **"SHADDAI EL CHAI"** (Shah-dye El-Chai) (meaning "Almighty Living God") several times as before. Continue to visualize the violet sphere strongly.

Next, visualize the shaft of light descending straight down from Yesod into your Malkuth center at the feet and ankles. Imagine a sphere of light formed there from the colors of citrine, russet brown, olive green and black. Vibrate the name **"ADONAI HA-ARTEZ"** (Ah-doe-nye Ha-Ah-retz) (meaning "Lord of Earth") a number of times as before. Maintain a strong visualization of the multi-colored sphere.

Imagine the Middle Pillar complete. Then circulate the light you have brought down through the Middle Pillar around the outside of your body to strengthen your aura. Using the cycles of breathing, bring the light up one side of the body and down the other, from Malkuth to Kether and back again. After performing this for a short period of time, imagine the ribbon of light descending down the front of your body and rising up your back.

Still employing rhythmic breathing, visualize the shaft of light rising up the Middle Pillar in the center of your body. When it reaches Kether, imagine a shower of light surrounding the outside of your body as it descends to Malkuth again. Circulate the light in this manner for some time. Then see the light rise again in a ribbon that spirals around the outside of your body.

Finally focus some of the energy back into your Tiphareth center, the seat of equilibrium and balance.

Advanced Color Workings

In addition to the exercise given above, color visualization can be used to work with the energies of one specific Sephirah for a given purpose. Both the King Scale and Queen Scale of colors can be used to this end.

For an example: Let's imagine that a student had trouble communicating and getting his ideas across to people. At that point, the student might decide to perform a spiritual exercise that would help him express himself better. Communication is attributed to the Sephirah of Hod, so that is the sphere the student would work with. Since he wants to *receive* the energies of Hod, he will use the Queen Scale color of Hod, which is orange. (Remember that the Queen Scale is feminine and therefore it is *receptive*. And in this case the student wishes to receive the benefit from this exercise—to make himself the vessel to be filled with Hod's power.)

To perform the exercise correctly, the student should have a lot of experience in performing the basic Middle Pillar Exercise. Persistent practice of this rite can provide great quantities of spiritual power, transforming the subconscious mind into a powerful storage battery that is ready to project or attract the Sephirotic power that is needed.

To begin, the student would first visualize the Queen Scale color of Hod, which is orange. He must focus and concentrate on this color until his entire aura is orange. He might also imagine every cell in his body bathed in an ocean of orange, or he could picture currents of orange light descending upon him from all directions. By using the Queen Scale color of orange, the Sephirah of Hod within the student's aura will be open, passive, and receptive.

Next, the student should then charge and vitalize the Sephirah of Hod within his aura by vibrating several times the divine name of Hod, which is **Elohim Tzabaoth.** He must vibrate the name until it seems as though all the forces in the Universe that are connected with Hod are drawn to him. Through persistent psychic work with this exercise, his powers of communication should improve.

In another example, suppose that the student knew someone else who had a communication problem. First the student should make certain that the individual with the problem wants outside psychic assistance, because it would be unethical to proceed otherwise.

If the help is welcomed, the student would begin by vibrating the name **Elohim Tzabaoth** and visualizing the color of Hod as before, but this time he would use Hod's King Scale color of violet. (Keep in mind that the King Scale is *masculine, active,* and *stimulating.* Therefore the student would use the color violet to actively project the energy of Hod to someone else.)

Instead of imagining the universal forces streaming toward himself, the student would visualize that these forces are awakened within him (by vibration and color) only to be projected from him to the person in need. If at the same time, the recipient assumes a meditative state, the effect will be even more powerful.

This method combines psychic suggestion with the willed concentration of vital power. Its success depends on one's skill and familiarity with the Kabbalistic system.

Archangels and Their Colors

The following is a list of all the archangels assigned to the Spheres on the Tree of Life, along with their corresponding colors. The robes, wings, and other items associated with each archangel can be visualized in the appropriate colors during meditation.

Sephirah	Archangel	Robe Colors
Kether	Metatron	White trimmed with black
Chokmah	Raziel	Gray trimmed with black or white
Binah	Tzaphqiel	Black trimmed with white
Chesed	Tzadqiel	Blue trimmed with orange
Geburah	Khamael	Red trimmed with green
Tiphareth	Raphael	Yellow trimmed with violet
Netzach	Haniel	Green trimmed with red

Hod	Michael	Orange trimmed with blue
Yesod	Gabriel	Violet trimmed with yellow
Malkuth	Sandalphon	Four Malkuth colors with white trim

The attributions of all of the Sephiroth can be used for bringing needed energy or influence to yourself or to others. The following is a list of attributes or qualities that each Sephirah can be used for.

Kether   Illumination, spirituality, peace, tranquillity, completion, synthesis, Divine Light.

Chokmah   Initiative, stimulating energy, vitalizing force, Divine Wisdom, Paternal Wisdom.

Binah   Secrets, Strength through silence, understanding of sorrows and burdens, organization, structuring, setting limits, faith, Maternal Understanding.

Chesed   Financial gain, abundance, prosperity, justice, fairness, new opportunities, obedience to higher, government, generosity, laughter, good outlook on life.

Geburah   Energy, courage, fortitude, change, getting rid of what is outmoded, cleansing, purifying, critical judgment, war and discord.

Tiphareth   Devotion, illumination, mystic visions, harmony, balance, glory, healing, life and success, Christ consciousness.

Netzach   Creativity, the arts, love and passion, social consciousness, idealism, sexuality, energy and understanding in relationships, unselfishness.

Hod   Communication, learning, teaching, writing, magic, ability to "wheel and deal," truthfulness, ability to detect falsehood, Journeying, commerce.

Yesod   Intuition, psychic abilities, dreams and visions, prophecies, mental health, independence, confidence, understanding of the cycles of change.

Malkuth   Materialization, environment, completion, physical health, overcoming inertia, self-discovery, discrimination.

The Tree Walk
A Guided Visualization

It is not our wish to exclude the solitary student from sharing in the experience of the Tree Walk simply because of a shortage of fellow participants. Therefore we have devised a simple way to adapt the speeches ("Addresses") from the Tree Walk with the Middle Pillar Exercise. The result is a combination of ritual and guided visualization that should convey the Tree Walk experience to one person or even a small number of individuals.

Begin by performing the Exercise of the Three Pillars, vibrating the divine names one time apiece to simulate the rushing energy of the Flaming Sword descending the Tree within your aura. Then pause for a few moments of relaxation and rhythmic breathing.

Next begin formulating the ascending path of return while vibrating the divine names in reverse order from Malkuth to Kether.

Malkuth

Imagine a sphere of light formed at your feet and ankles in the colors of citrine, russet brown, olive green, and black. Vibrate the name **"ADONAI HA-ARTEZ"** a number of times. Then visualize the Sephirotic guide of Malkuth as described in Chapter Two. Read or listen to the Address of Malkuth also taken from Chapter Two. (Note: another person can read the appropriate speeches to you, or you can pre-record yourself reciting the speeches.)

Yesod

Visualize a sphere of violet light formed at the genital region. Intone the name **"SHADDAI EL CHAI"** several times as before. Then imagine the Sephirotic guide of Yesod as described in Chapter Two. Read or listen to the Address of Yesod taken from that section of the book.

Hod

Imagine a sphere of orange light at the area of your right hip. Vibrate the name **"ELOHIM TZABAOTH"** several times. Then visualize the Sephirotic guide of Hod as described in Chapter Two. Read or listen to the Address of Hod as described earlier.

Netzach

Visualize a sphere of green light at the area of your left hip. Vibrate the name **"YHVH TZABAOTH"** a number of times. Then imagine the Sephirotic guide of Netzach as described in Chapter Two. Read or listen to the Address of Netzach.

Tiphareth

Imagine a sphere of yellow light around the area of your heart. Vibrate the name **"YHVH ELOAH VE-DAATH"** several times. Then visualize the Sephirotic guide of Tiphareth as described in Chapter Two. Read or listen to the Address of Tiphareth.

Geburah

Imagine a sphere of red light at your right shoulder. Vibrate the name **"ELOHIM GIBOR"** a number of times. Then imagine the Sephirotic guide of Geburah as described in Chapter Two. Read or listen to the Address of Geburah.

Chesed

Visualize a sphere of blue light at your left shoulder. Vibrate the name **"EL"** a number of times. Then imagine the Sephirotic guide of Chesed as described in Chapter Two. Read or listen to the Address of Chesed.

Binah

Imagine a sphere of black light at the right temple of your forehead. Vibrate the name **"YHVH ELOHIM"** several times. Then visualize the Sephirotic guide of Binah as described in Chapter Two. Read or listen to the Address of Binah.

Chokmah

Visualize a sphere of gray light at the left temple of your forehead. Intone the name of **"YAH"** several times. Then visualize the Sephirotic guide of Chokmah as described in Chapter Two. Read or listen to the Address of Chokmah.

Kether

Imagine a sphere of white light just above your head. Vibrate the name **"EHEIEH"** a number of times. Then see the white sphere open out into a pyramid of white light that surrounds you on all sides. Imagine a mirror in front of you, where you see your own face reflected. A voice tells you, "Behold the face of God." Then you see what appears to be the image of a candle flame—a single spark of fire—the point of origin for all that is. The point of flame becomes a spinning galaxy of stars.

Meditate on the vision for as long as you like, then finish the exercise by circulating the light with the rhythmic cycles of breathing as in the basic Middle Pillar rite. At the very end, focus some of the energy back into your Tiphareth center for balance and equilibrium.

Affirmations

The following affirmations can be a daily reminder of the student's spiritual quest for divine knowledge, balance, and wisdom. There are seven affirmations per Sephirah, and of these, the student should concentrate on one per day. Throughout the course of a day, the phrase should be remembered and contemplated. This will help focus the mind on the importance of bringing the spiritual into the routines of daily life.

Kether

1. I am a living channel for the Divine Light.
2. I am the source of all peace.
3. I am all that is.
4. I am the completion of the journey.
5. I am because I am.
6. I am the beginning and the end.
7. There is no part of me that is not of God.

Chokmah

1. I initiate.
2. I am the Father of all Fathers.
3. I am the divine spark of life.
4. I am the moving force of the universe.
5. True wisdom is all-powerful.
6. Wisdom is a gift given to the wise.
7. There is no higher wisdom than mine.

Binah

1. I organize.
2. I am pure faith.
3. I am the secret of secrets.
4. I am the Mother of all Mothers.
5. I am the understanding of sorrow.
6. There is truth in silence.
7. Strength through silence is my name.

Chesed

1. I am eternal love.
2. I am always willing to forgive.
3. My hand is always fair and just.
4. I give abundance in all things.
5. I understand the need for obedience to the Higher.
6. Laughter is my song of praise.
7. The first duty of a king is to serve.

Geburah

1. I am the holy warrior.
2. I uphold the authority of the Divine.
3. I overcome all obstacles in my path.
4. I am a purifying Fire.
5. I stand, bravely and justly.
6. My judgment is critical.
7. Through the strength of God shall I prevail.

Tiphareth

1. I am the way, the truth, and the life.
2. I am the healer.
3. I walk the path of the mystic.
4. Look from without to within.
5. I always strive for the highest.

6. Balance is the key.

7. There is beauty all around me.

Netzach

1. I walk with the grace of God.

2. I dare to dream.

3. I fan the fires of inspiration.

4. My victory is in God.

5. I am the heart of love.

6. The desire for my Lord has consumed me.

7. All adorations to God are my songs.

Hod

1. I am the teacher.

2. I wish to know.

3. I seek truth.

4. I listen.

5. I hear God's word.

6. I am the journeyman on the path.

7. Know thyself.

Yesod

1. I uphold the universe.

2. I created humanity.

3. I am the foundation of time and space.

4. I am the creator of dreams.

5. I ebb and flow.

6. I can see the future, the present, and the past.

7. I cause the cycles of change.

Malkuth

1. I am the gate to the Garden of Eden.

2. I am God made manifest.

3. I am the completion of the divine plan.

4. I choose wisely, with discrimination.

5. I am the unfolding of the Light.

6. I am the kingdom.

7. I am made in the image of the Divine.

Endnotes

1. Several variations of this exercise are given in the book *The Middle Pillar: The Balance Between Mind and Magic* by Israel Regardie with new material provided by ourselves.

2. Daath is not properly a Sephirah, but can be likened to a bridge or passageway across the Abyss, which is a boundary between the higher Sephiroth (Kether, Chokmah, and Binah), and the lower seven spheres on the tree. The divine names of Binah are normally assigned to Daath, because Binah is the closest of the Supernals to Daath, and it is Binah whose powers are seen reflected through Daath to the lower parts of the tree.

3. All the colors can be found on page 99 of Israel Regardie's *The Golden Dawn* (Sixth Edition, Llewellyn Publications).

4. In diagrams that show the Sephiroth and the paths that connect them in color, the Sephiroth are tinted in the Queen Scale, while the Paths, which are energy conduits, are given in the King Scale. The Paths, as a whole, are regarded as male. They are the stimulating and active outpourings of force in motion.

BIBLIOGRAPHY

Cicero, Chic, and Sandra Tabatha Cicero. *Self-Initiation into the Golden Dawn Tradition*. St. Paul, MN: Llewellyn Publications, 1995.

Compton, Madonna. *Archetypes on the Tree of Life*, Third Edition. St. Paul, MN: Llewellyn Publications, 1991.

Godwin, David. *Godwin's Cabalistic Encyclopedia*, Third Edition. St. Paul, MN: Llewellyn Publications, 1994.

Greer, John Michael. *Pathways of Wisdom*. St. Paul, MN: Publications, 1996.

Halevi, Z'ev ben Shimon. *Kabbalah: Tradition of Hidden Knowledge*. New York, NY: Thames and Hudson, 1988.

Knight, Gareth. *A Practical Guide to Qabalistic Symbolism*. York Beach, ME: Samuel Weiser, Inc., 1983.

Regardie, Israel. *The Art of True Healing*. San Rafael, CA: New World Library, 1991.

Regardie, Israel. *The Golden Dawn*, Sixth Edition. St. Paul, MN: Llewellyn Publications, 1994.

Regardie, Israel. *The Middle Pillar*, Second Edition. St. Paul, MN: Llewellyn Publications, 1994.

Sepher Yetzirah. Translated by William Wynn Westcott. Edmonds, WA: Holmes Publishing Group, 1996

Wang, Robert. *The Qabalistic Tarot.* York Beach, ME: Samuel Weiser, Inc., 1983.

INDEX

LOOK FOR THE CRESCENT MOON

Llewellyn publishes hundreds of books on your favorite subjects! To get these exciting books, including the ones on the following pages, check your local bookstore or order them directly from Llewellyn.

ORDER BY PHONE

- Call toll-free within the U.S. and Canada, 1-800-THE MOON
- In Minnesota, call (612) 291-1970
- We accept VISA, MasterCard, and American Express

ORDER BY MAIL

- Send the full price of your order (MN residents add 7% sales tax) in U.S. funds, plus postage & handling to:

    Llewellyn Worldwide
    P.O. Box 64383, Dept. (K 138-4)
    St. Paul, MN 55164–0383, U.S.A.

POSTAGE & HANDLING

(For the U.S., Canada, and Mexico)

- $4 for orders $15 and under
- $5 for orders over $15
- No charge for orders over $100

We ship UPS in the continental United States. We ship standard mail to P.O. boxes. Orders shipped to Alaska, Hawaii, The Virgin Islands, and Puerto Rico are sent first-class mail. Orders shipped to Canada and Mexico are sent surface mail.

International orders: Airmail—add freight equal to price of each book to the total price of order, plus $5.00 for each non-book item (audio tapes, etc.).

Surface mail—Add $1.00 per item.

Allow 4–6 weeks for delivery on all orders.
Postage and handling rates subject to change.

DISCOUNTS

We offer a 20% discount to group leaders or agents. You must order a minimum of 5 copies of the same book to get our special quantity price.

FREE CATALOG

Get a free copy of our color catalog, *New Worlds of Mind and Spirit*. Subscribe for just $10.00 in the United States and Canada ($30.00 overseas, airmail). Many bookstores carry *New Worlds*—ask for it!

Visit our website at www.llewellyn.com for more information.

THE GOLDEN DAWN JOURNAL
BOOK ONE: DIVINATION
edited by Chic Cicero and
Sandra Tabatha Cicero

The Golden Dawn Journal is an ongoing series of books designed to reflect the magical teachings and philosophy of the Hermetic Tradition. The books will seriously explore the techniques used in ceremonial magick and include practical ritual advice for the working magician. Each volume will focus on one theme, with contributions by various authors experienced in Western ceremonial magic.

Book One: Divination explores how and why the process of divination works, traditional techniques of Tarot and Geomancy (along with new information on both), new Tarot spreads, historical information derived from the actual Tarot readings of an original member of th Golden Dawn, explorations of both Roman and Græco-Egyptian divinatory techniques, Gypsy Runes, and new systems of divination developed by accomplished magicians in the field. All authors then respond to the question, "Can a Divination Always Be Trusted?"

As both an order and a Magickal Tradition, the Golden Dawn is responsible for planting many of the seeds of Magick that have sprouted today in the form of numerous Magickal organizations throughout the world.

1-56718-850-8, 304 pp., 6 x 9, softcover   **$12.00**

To order, call 1-800-THE MOON
Prices subject to change without notice

**THE CRAFTING & USE OF
RITUAL TOOLS**
*Step-by-Step Instructions for
Woodcrafting Religious &
Magical Implements*
Eleanor and Philip Harris

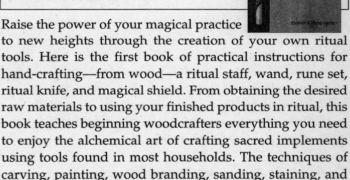

Raise the power of your magical practice
to new heights through the creation of your own ritual
tools. Here is the first book of practical instructions for
hand-crafting—from wood—a ritual staff, wand, rune set,
ritual knife, and magical shield. From obtaining the desired
raw materials to using your finished products in ritual, this
book teaches beginning woodcrafters everything you need
to enjoy the alchemical art of crafting sacred implements
using tools found in most households. The techniques of
carving, painting, wood branding, sanding, staining, and
applying finish are explained in a simple "how-to" format.

From materials pulsing with the energy of nature, you
can hand-craft implements of equal or better quality than
the more expensive ones available for purchase. What's
more, you can infuse them with your own personal energy,
making them a sacred extension of your unique beliefs,
practices, and personal symbolism.

1-56718-346-8, 6 x 9, 264 pp.   **$14.95**

To order, call 1-800-THE MOON
Prices subject to change without notice

A KABBALAH FOR THE MODERN WORLD
Migene González-Wippler

A Kabbalah for the Modern World was the first book to present the Kabbalah from a scientific orientation and show how it clearly relates to such modern scientific models as Quantum Theory, Relativity and the Big Bang. Now this Kabbalah classic has been revised and expanded to include a larger bibliography and new section: The Kabbalah of Wisdom. This new section includes never before published information and rituals, making this fascinating book more important than ever!

This book is not merely a "magical manual." It is far more than that. It is a journey into new dimensions of being, self-discovery and spiritual development. Above all, it is a search for "devekkut," the true union with the Godhead. Reading *A Kabbalah for the Modern World* is a unique experience. You will grow inwardly as you read, as your spirit comprehends the message ... and you will never, ever be the same again.

0-87542-294-2, 304 pp. 5¼ x 8, softcover   **$12.95**

To order, call 1-800-THE MOON
Prices subject to change without notice